W9-AUI-628

What Industry Experts are Saying About How To Build a Successful 401(k) and Retirement Plan Advisory Business

"...Enter into their earnest, broad discussion. You will be changed by taking seriously the Chalk-Barlow challenges, generated by their special retirement plan market experiences.

— Kristine J. Coffey, CPC
Executive Vice President, CPE Associates
Financial Services Management and Consulting Since 1975

"This is a thought-provoking manual written specifically for the consultant/advisor willing to undertake the rigor and thought necessary to position their business for maximum success."

— Mark B. Robinson CIMA®, AIF®,
Ferris, Baker, Watts, Inc.
Member NYSE SIPC
Host of "The Careful Capitalist" radio show

How To Build
A Successful
401(k) and
Retirement Plan
Advisory Business

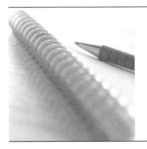

A Step-By-Step Guide
to Maximizing Your
Business Potential

Steff C. Chalk
Christopher H. Barlow

© 2005 Steff Chalk & Christopher Barlow

All rights reserved. Printed in the United States of America. No part of this book may be used or reproduced in any manner without written permission of the authors.

Library of Congress Control Number: 2005910814

ISBN: 0-9776618-0-6

Design by Susan Kandzer Design

Contents

Section I – Defining Your Brand

Section II – Product Awareness

Section III – Continuous Improvement

Section IV – Your Responsibility

Section V – Maximum Efficiency

Appendix

Acknowledgements

From Steff Chalk

In early 1980 my career took a turn that would forever change my life — I moved from the computer division of a financial services company to the investment division. What a profound and pleasant event that turned out to be.

Much of what is presented here is the result of my having spent over 25 years in the financial services industry. Over the course of my career there have been thousands who have provided (and who continue to provide) me with vast and valuable insight into the retirement plan industry. Under the tutelage of these investment advisors, plan sponsors, registered representatives, attorneys, third party administrators, and trust-bankers, I have acquired a diverse and intricate knowledge of our domestic retirement industry and the social retirement issues faced by countries less bountiful than the United States of America.

I extend a special thank you to those individuals who, during my career, have in some special way guided, supported or taught me. They include non-industry friends who have provided me with unwavering support for many, many years, and industry professionals who I also consider good friends, who have shared their extensive knowledge and guided me along the right path by their own behavior and actions. They are: Bill Keating, Jr., Barry Babbitt, Steve Scudder, Alper Toper, Marshall Esler, Billy Spearman, Nadia El Shafie, Bob Burneka, Ralph Waldvogel, Mike Madden, Andy Sweeny, Bob Costello and Bob Spearman.

I wish to thank my co-author, an industry leader and my friend, Chris Barlow, who convinced me that we possessed the knowledge that industry professionals want and that we should write this book. This book would not exist without Chris' persistence and encouragement.

Thank you to my parents and sister, who have supported me unconditionally over the years. And thank you to Cindy, my wife, who has been more than patient with the hours I have spent writing and concentrating on this work. She continues to encourage me to pursue my dreams.

In having all of the above industry contacts, friends and family, I am truly blessed.

From Chris Barlow

I wish to first acknowledge the skill, thought and dedication that Steff Chalk brought to the creation of this work. I also want to thank Steff for encouraging me to look at the world of Financial Advisors serving the 401(k)/Company Retirement Plan marketplace in new and challenging ways.

I want to thank my Mom, who passed away in 2005. She showed me how to live a productive and meaningful life through helping others.

My wife continually provides a loving and nurturing environment for me to accomplish endeavors large and small, and my daughters have proved to be uniquely capable of keeping me focused on what is truly important in life.

And finally to the tens of thousands of Financial Advisors who have taught and challenged me over the years. I wish you all Continued Success!

From Both of Us

Three special individuals shared their time with us, above and beyond our expectations. We are fortunate and grateful to know them as both business associates and great friends. They are true industry pioneers and professionals. Our special thanks to them — Ted Benna, Kristine Coffey and Fred Reisch. They generously undertook to read our manuscript in its entirety, through business crunches and vacations. Each made valuable contributions and suggestions. Their contributions are greatly appreciated as they have helped to make this book everything we wanted it to be.

Steff and Chris

Introduction

Your business is unique, even if the products, services and systems you offer are not. What you do, how you do it, and why you do it — are all directed by you. This gives you a perfect insider position from which to objectively analyze your business with an eye towards improving it. And chances are, even if business is good, it can be made better. It is unlikely that anyone in the retirement plan universe is the best in every aspect. Perfection is an elusive ideal. But improvement is not. So now what? Ask yourself this question: "Do I have a plan for making my organization better than the competition?"

If you do not have a plan, we think it is time to consider getting one! We have been helping Financial Advisors, investment consultants, third party administrators, insurance producers and benefits brokers to improve their businesses for a combined total of forty years. During our business careers we have worked closely with hundreds of Financial Advisor related businesses. A few were great, a few were terrible and most were somewhere in between. But they all benefited from a little hard-nosed analysis and the application of a well-conceived action plan. When appropriately applied, the concepts, principles and structures presented in this book will get you remarkably close to what we call Maximum Efficiency^{SM}.

Maximum Efficiency should be thought of as a state of being, a continuous process rather than a static point in the business maturation process. We believe that any business (process, division or unit) can always be improved. To cease improvement is to concede that the competition can ultimately deliver better, faster, cheaper or more efficiently than you. You should continually reach for the ever-elusive final rung on the process improvement ladder. The most successful teams continually reach for Maximum Efficiency.

As soon as you feel that you have "arrived" at Maximum Efficiency, be certain that you have not! It should forever remain elusive and never be attained — for every Financial Advisor. That assures continuous improvement!

Perspective

Since the inception of the Social Security system, most Americans have depended upon their government or employers to structure and fund their retirement savings. This is especially true for those who do not have the awareness or resources to save on their own, or for those who have suffered economic catastrophe. It was not until the Individual Retirement Account (IRA) was introduced in 1975 that employees who were not covered by any employer-sponsored retirement savings plan could establish one, contribute to it and deduct their contribution from their taxes. Since 1975, major revisions to the federal tax code and changes to Social Security have drastically altered the retirement funding landscape. Unquestionably, the most dramatic revision to retirement planning and delivery has been the opportunity for American workers to make their own decisions about meeting their retirement needs. Actually, the 401(k) plan emerged through a loophole of the Tax Reform Act passed in 1978. In 1981, the Internal Revenue Service granted provisional approval to Theodore (Ted) Benna for the establishment of the first 401(k) plan. Since the opening of that first 401(k) plan, the 401(k) structure and traditional defined benefit and defined contribution plans have amassed assets totaling in excess of $13 trillion. The 401(k) has become a powerful retirement savings tool that provides a disciplined, pre-tax, often matched, and tax-deferred compounded return on money invested. The traditional defined benefit and defined contribution plans are company retirement plans sponsored by the employer. We think that the 401(k) plan will continue as the retirement plan option of choice for both employers and wage earners.

The evolution of the retirement savings system in the United States

Any discussion of the history of retirement savings in the United States has to include a reference to the Social Security "leg" of the "three legged stool" (the other two being employer-sponsored plans and personal savings). Social Security's official name is Old-Age, Survivors, and

Disability Insurance (OASDI). It was created and amended through the years as a way to alleviate, via "social insurance," poverty ensuing from old age, retirement, death of an income earning spouse or parent or disability to an income earner. It is structured to collect wealth from those who generate taxable income and redistribute a portion of that wealth to those who receive Social Security benefits.

The roots of Social Security can be traced to Otto von Bismarck's Germany, where in 1883 the Sickness Insurance Law was enacted, followed in 1884 with the Accident Insurance Law, and in 1889 with the Old Age and Disability Insurance Law. German lawmakers were putting in place "social insurance" programs in an effort to forestall the rise of socialism in the land of Karl Marx.

In the United States, economic conditions including multiple stock market crashes and the Great Depression created a ripe environment for the grass roots movement that proposed ways for our nation to care for our elderly. The Townsend Movement began in 1933 and added tremendous political pressure on Congress to act. On August 14, 1935, Franklin D. Roosevelt signed the Social Security Act into law.

Through the years amendments were made to expand eligibility, increase benefits, raise payroll taxes and later to decrease benefits for early retirement. Future changes to maintain the solvency of Social Security may involve raising payroll (FICA) taxes, raising the retirement age, and/or reducing benefits, and possibly allowing taxpayers to manage a portion or all of their FICA contributions.

Our view on Social Security

At this writing the estimated shortfall for The United States Social Security is in excess of $10 trillion. According to the Social Security Trustee's 2004 and 2005 reports, every single year that we postpone funding the system will result in an additional $600 billion shortfall.

Social Security was designed many decades ago under very different circumstances for the primary purpose of reducing poverty, but has since come to be seen as a default "retirement plan." The demographics and the government's deficit funding of the "Trust Fund," disabuse most informed Americans of any notion that our existing "pay-as-you-go" system is sustainable for very much longer. Given American voting patterns, most politicians lack the courage to make the changes necessary to maintain the solvency of the Social Security system. They also seem to lack the imagination required to enact more "modern" approaches to accumulating wealth in our social structure. Some of these requisite progressive measures have already been enacted in Chile, Sweden, and Turkey as well as in other countries.

There can be no doubt that future retirees face a vastly different set of circumstances than their parents did. Every American deserves financial security in retirement or disability. Recent historical trends seem to indicate a strong shift to the private sector for retirement programs. There is a lot of opportunity, so we should immediately look to the future and begin moving forward.

Why do employers sponsor retirement plans at their companies?

There is no law mandating that employers sponsor any employee benefit program, including 401(k), so why would an employer do so? Employers have sponsored and maintained retirement plans at their companies primarily to reward themselves and valued employees. However, they also realize that such plans can create beneficial recruitment advantages. With an eye on their company's profitability, these programs are used as inducements to acquire and retain quality, productive employees. Like most business decisions, it is generally driven by the bottom line.

What objectives does an employer usually have when they install a 401(k) Plan?

Employers want a program in which the burden on the employer is minimized and the benefit to the employee is maximized. Remember that the employer is not in business to provide retirement benefits. All employers are in business to generate a profit by assembling a product or providing a service.

What should 401(k) plans deliver?

401(k) plans should deliver a competitive advantage to employers by providing their employees with a superior retirement benefit. For you, the Financial Advisor, it provides the opportunity to generate immediate and ongoing compensation while enhancing and deepening relationships with clients.

What should be your focus and what is your role in the 401(k)/Company Retirement Plan market?

As the Financial Advisor, you have to decide what you want your role to be. Do you want to simply be an order taker or do you want to serve the 401(k) market to the fullest? Or will you choose to be somewhere in between? The more services offered, the greater the reward. Wherever you choose to focus, wherever your niche may lie, you must be committed to the delivery of exceptional service to both employers and employees. That is the bottom line for controlling your own success.

Will you operate as a Registered Representative or as a Registered Investment Advisor?

Over the past several years a growing discussion and, in some instances, debate, has ensued among 401(k)/Company Retirement Plan industry professionals concerning what is the best, most competitive role for Financial Advisors and investment consultants. The agenda items are far-reaching but the true focal point of these conversations revolves around the topics of compensation and fiduciary concerns. The resulting issue becomes how (and with whom) you are registered.

Registered Representatives are regulated by the NASD (National Association of Securities Dealers). With the exception of wrap accounts, their allegiance lies with their clearing broker dealer. The registered representative typically does not contractually serve as a fiduciary to the plan sponsor. The registered representative is compensated on a commission basis or some derivation of a commission on the transaction.

Registered Investment Advisors are regulated by the SEC (Securities and Exchange Commission). Their allegiance is to the plan sponsor. A registered investment advisor serves in a fiduciary capacity to the plan fiduciaries and plan participants. The registered investment advisor has flexibility in how they can be compensated for their services, provided the compensation structure is disclosed in the Securities and Exchange Commission's Form ADV.

Will employer-sponsored plans continue to exist?

Despite the recently revealed failings and, in a few cases, outright fraud within some employer-sponsored retirement plans, the outlook for growth in company sponsored retirement plans seems assured. If future tax laws continue to favor the formation of employer-sponsored retirement savings plans, the Employee Retirement Income Security Act (ERISA) enforcement policies will address the need to keep fiduciaries fiscally responsible. Though future tax laws and the status of Social Security are always unknown, the competitive pressures of free enterprise and the imperative of governments to control spending should sustain the employer-sponsored retirement savings market. Investors also want more control over their retirement funds. As long as employers want to be profitable and employees want to retire yesterday, there will be a growing market for you to serve that generates revenue for your business.

What if our tax laws change and there are no longer 401(k) plans as we know them today?

Should tax laws be designed to influence our behavior or simply to raise revenue? Should government provide complete retirement security to everyone or just those who can not provide it for themselves? Should government be involved at all? These and other perplexing questions will persist for some time. So, if changes in tax laws and policy do eliminate the 401(k), would any other program take their place? And if so, what would those new programs look like?

We are quite certain that the "baby boomers," "baby busters," "Gen-Xers" and all other concerned Americans will continue to demand an opportunity to save for their own retirement, preferably on a tax deferred basis. They may be comfortable with an approach that does not involve their employers. The "new" opportunity may involve managing their FICA-Social Security savings (assuming Social Security is still around). Would this new system offer tax incentives and features such as before-tax contributions, tax-deferred compounding and tax-efficient distribution options? No one knows.

There are many questions, and before any decisions are made, there will be extensive debate. Your focus should be on the possible impact to your business if the 401(k)/Company Retirement Plan rug is pulled out from under you. There will be plenty of warning. Stay current with changing tax laws. Be prepared to take advantage of the opportunities if such change occurs.

There will always be retirement assets — those previously accumulated and those yet to be. So opportunities are certain to be plentiful. Whatever occurs in the market, ensure that you are the one your client turns to for answers. Be in a position to guide them through any change that may come. Your many competitors will be afforded the same advance warning, yet some will choose to resist, to defend the status quo, only to be swamped when the inevitable tide of change comes. Be prepared for it and you can surf your way to success.

What are the advantages for Financial Advisors who serve the 401(k) market?

- Provides a consistent and growing income stream from the automatic and systematic contributions and tax-deferred growth of the assets
- Creates new business relationships with access to additional sources of business and compensation
- Retains and deepens existing relationships
- Enhances the reputation as a knowledgeable industry resource

How To Use This Book

The intention of this book is twofold — to deliver information and to provoke thought. Portions of the book are entirely narrative — the reader is presented data, concepts and other information. Throughout the book are targeted, specific questions. The questions are posed in the interest of assisting the reader in identifying strong and weak areas of their own business.

The book is intended as a roadmap to success, not a "silver bullet" solution. We have invested extensive time in gathering and refining the processes and methodologies that assist Financial Advisors in improving their skills, and ultimately their results. Ideally, the book will be used as a tool for taking your retirement plan business to the next level, and beyond. Your efforts must be focused specifically on reaching a higher level of performance that we describe as Maximum Efficiency[SM].

The book is divided into five distinct sections (Defining Your Brand, Product Awareness, Continuous Improvement, Your Responsibility and Maximum Efficiency). Some readers might choose to skip one section or another, or they might go directly to the section that addresses their primary concern.

One of the inherent challenges associated with attempting to transfer knowledge in writing is a book's linear construction. The progression of chapters within a book can give the impression that earlier chapters are either more important than the subsequent chapters or that they stand completely on their own, isolated from the rest. Within this book nothing could be further from the truth. You will notice similar concepts and methodologies appearing throughout the book, applied to the topic of that chapter. To emphasize the point, although it is an excellent medium for sharing information and ideas, the linear structure of a book requires that you accept the ideas and concepts in a specific order. That order may not be best for you. We encourage you to move through the chapters in an order that will deliver the most benefit to you. (When we consult with Financial Advisor teams in person, we have the luxury of not being restricted to a linear flow.)

We have arranged this book as a dialogue in question and answer format. Typical reader questions appear in bold italic text and we provide the answers to them. Some questions we put to you to stimulate your thought process and help clarify the current status of your business. These appear in bold text and many are highlighted with this graphic. Considering all questions thoroughly and responding to each one accurately will help you choose how to successfully manage your 401(k)/ Retirement Plan advisory business.

Treat this like a textbook. Always have a pen in-hand. Feel free to highlight, underline and use the margins for notes. In some sections it will be helpful to have a notepad as well. The notepad is not a requirement, but reading the book with pen in-hand is! Your notes will assist you in developing both structure and process to your Brand, Strategy and Vision — and much more.

Finally, if you have any questions or comments concerning the content of this text please feel free to e-mail us at steffchalk@aol.com or empowering@knowhow401k.com It is our hope that you will enjoy your journey to Maximum Efficiency!

Section I – Defining Your Brand

1

Self-Assessment

The first step in building a successful 401(k)/Company Retirement Plan business is defining your brand. But in the absence of a multi-million dollar public relations and advertising budget, just how do you go about it?

We have worked with many Financial Advisors and financial services teams to help them define their brand and improve their business. When we first meet with them we ask a lot of questions to take inventory of their beliefs and behaviors. Thought-provoking and insightful questions, when considered and answered honestly, provide the appropriate perspective for us to best assist our clients in the further development of their business. We refer to this extremely important time as the assessment period. The responses, after assembly, analysis and organization, become the foundation upon which the Financial Advisor operates. The assessment period is the time for asking pointed questions, answering those questions and, with the assistance of your team members, if applicable, defining major initiatives for building your 401(k)/Company Retirement Plan business. Taking an introspective yet objective look at your activities and results will help you to obtain an accurate assessment of your business.

This section contains specific, targeted questions to get you started. Grab a pen and a notepad because as you progress through these questions there will be information and insights that you will want to record. Many of your responses will serve as input to your strategic plan, business plans, marketing plans, goals and objectives.

The most important thing to keep in mind is that, in this business, the brand is YOU!

Introspection

Q. 1   What did you do before becoming a Financial Advisor?

Earlier life experiences have shaped who you are today and have an incredible impact on what you can expect to accomplish in the future. Look at yourself and take an accurate inventory of the good, the bad and the ugly. If you resemble most Financial Advisors, you probably possess at least some of each. All life experiences — financial and non-financial — are useful if you allow them to be. Part of your never-ending challenge is successfully communicating your knowledgeable perspective and unique process to your plan sponsor prospects. You need to accurately convey evidence of how you are the best option for a prospect compared to your competition. Your personal and professional experiences are the basis of your product.

Take a moment to mentally reference your resume, bio or CV.

 WRITE IT
Be sure to include everything that has contributed to making you who you have become. We recommend an outline form here.

Q. 2   What experiences (both personal and professional) are "milestones" that define you?

All of us have accumulated experiences that have shaped us into who we are. Taking inventory of past experience provides the context to grow. Thinking of your milestones will boost your confidence as you move through self-assessment.

 WRITE IT

Q. 3   What past career experiences will assist you in the role of a Financial Advisor?

Your clients are looking to you to assist them in making sound financial decisions concerning their retirement plans. Strong analytical skills, strong communication skills and a dose of healthy curiosity are a few ingredients that may be part of your past. These and any other business related experiences should be "packaged" into who you are and what you can offer the client.

 WRITE IT
(We again suggest an outline form.)

Q. 4 What is your annual 401(k)/Company Retirement Plan Business revenue?

Either as a sole producer or part of a team, establishing the revenue base is important. It is impossible to measure progress without a thorough knowledge of current revenue. This is a non-optional exercise if you are serious about getting better in the retirement plan market. Be honest with yourself and the team. State your revenue accurately. (This exercise, just like most of the exercises in this book, is focused on serving and growing retirement plan business. The same strategies and techniques can be applied to a diversified business including wealth management, non-qualified plans or business/corporate services. Such diversification increases the opportunity for future growth of your overall revenue.)

 WRITE IT

Q. 5 Prepare an inventory of your current 401(k)/Company Retirement Plans, and all other employer-sponsored retirement savings plans.

To obtain the best information available (upon which to base future business decisions and ultimately create your successful 401(k)/ Company Retirement Plan business) we suggest that you have an understanding of the following:

- Type of plans (401(k), defined benefit, profit sharing, etc.)
- Industry segments you serve (i.e. Is all of your business with physicians? Are you concentrated in real estate firms, or food companies? Do you serve a specific niche? If you have an indus-

try-specific client base, take advantage of it. Consider positioning yourself in that industry, and build on it!)

- Year acquired (Obtain the average tenure and longest tenure of
  the plans that you serve.)
- Total 401(k) and Retirement Plan assets you serve (both)
- Number of eligible employees in your largest plan
- Total number of eligible employees in your care

 WRITE IT
We hope that you need a large notepad for this one!

Q. 6   In what percentage of your current 401(k)/Company Retirement Plan business was there a prior relationship with the decision maker(s) and or company?

This becomes a valuable nugget of information when you are establishing a business strategy.

Relationships have always been (and, we predict, will always be)
"king." As long as humans are involved in sales and decision-making
processes, relationships will play an important part in determining
who is chosen to serve the 401(k) plan market. While developing business outside of existing relationships is obviously a good idea, the
answer to this question may reveal to you the many opportunities
available to you in further developing existing relationships.

 WRITE IT

Q. 7   What are the primary reasons you were successful in winning your current plans?

Honesty here will serve you best. Brutally honest answers will reveal a
lot about your business and who you are.

 WRITE IT
Hopefully your answer here is not "having the lowest fees!"
Such a marketing strategy is destined to be rendered worth-
less by the next competitor who will gladly undercut your

pricing. Prepare and examine a list of benefits that you offer to the client. Devote special attention to those items over which you have some degree of control.

Q. 8 Describe the structure of your business (solo or team or something else). If you have a team, outline/describe team member responsibilities.

For sole practitioners with no assistant this response is simple — you do everything! For the rest of you, defining roles and responsibilities of team members can be a most challenging exercise — but it brings forth powerful information and benefits. Our experience is that roles and responsibilities are frequently too loosely defined and rarely documented. You can begin this exercise by jotting down a few names and a few lines beside each name. Eventually the answer to this question can be developed into a powerful tool for the successful Financial Advisor or team. (If you skip this question or feel that it is of little value, then you are missing something big! Poorly defined responsibilities frequently lead to poor accountability. Everyone should know their responsibilities and be held accountable for the overall results.)

WRITE IT

This can be a tough exercise, especially with a large team. But given the appropriate time and effort, this exercise can pay huge dividends. A valuable follow-up is to have all of the people on your team conduct the same exercise and then compare the results. You will be amazed at what you learn.

Q. 9 Do you have a current Business Plan?

This one is simple — the answer is either "yes" or "no." If you have a Business Plan, but you need to "dust it off," then it is not current. We will further develop this question in Chapter Four.

WRITE IT

If your answer is "yes," it will simplify your efforts. If your answer is "no," and you have no Business Plan, then you are in the same response category as most of your competitors. Now is the time to leave them behind!

Q. 10 Do you feel that you fully understand all that you (or your team) have to offer and deliver to clients — all of the talents and resources that each of your team members can provide?

You and your team members are assets. These assets should be appreciating in value over the years — are yours? Unfortunately "human capital assets" are frequently underutilized, or woefully ill-equipped to assist in the mission of the team. Know your team's position here.

WRITE IT

Knowing your position is a valuable step in progressing in the 401(k)/Company Retirement Plan business. This business is dramatically more labor intensive and complex than selling a mutual fund or trading a stock. In return, the 401(k)/ Company Retirement Plan business can be more satisfying and substantially more rewarding financially.

Q. 11 What monumental obstacles keep you from being a success in your job?

We all have obstacles that hinder the efficient execution of our job responsibilities. These obstacles can all be divided into two categories:

- Obstacles that you can control
- Obstacles that you cannot control

Take some time with this one and avoid the temptation to simply jot a few things down to fill space and move on. We frequently see Financial Advisors who initially provide only a surface answer to this question. It is not uncommon to have the real impediments revealed after a lengthy conversation. You must be willing to have that heart-to-heart internal conversation prior to responding here. We are confident that most Financial Advisors who take a serious interest in their own success can identify the true obstacles they face in their business.

WRITE IT

Now that you have listed these obstacles, return to the list and make sure that you have concentrated only on those that can be considered monumental. If you have too many, identify the biggest and work on those. You can address only a limited number of obstacles at any one time.

Now review the list for those obstacles that are under your control — those that you can remove. Systemic obstacles that emanate from corporate headquarters or industry regulation do not deserve your time and attention (unless you can have a meaningful impact on removing them.)

The biggest obstacles that you can identify and remove will provide you with the highest increased efficiency.

Q. 12 What are your exceptional skills?

Chances are that if you are exceptionally skilled at a particular service or task, then you enjoy performing within that arena. If you are a standout and enjoy doing it, then you need to effectively communicate your success. You probably have conviction. Conviction "sells" and breeds success. List those areas in which you are exceptional. Do not list the things that you perform well or adequately — just those that you perform exceptionally well. Do not be humble or bashful here. Go for it. List them.

 WRITE IT

Q. 13 What makes you or your team different than the competition?

Surely you have been asked this question many times. Before you answer, consider the last three times you have been asked this question. Do you always answer with the same response? Do you always tell people the exact same thing? If you are the leader of a team, does your entire team respond with the same answer to this question? Take a moment to write your response.

 WRITE IT

Your response can reflect your passion. Your response can show what is important to you. Your response is telling. Is it consistent? If it is not, then make it consistent. Is it always the same or usually the same? Do all team members share your Vision? Whenever asked this question, every member of the team should be able to give essentially the same response.

Q. 14 What are your greatest opportunities for improvement in the 401(k)/Company Retirement Plan marketplace?

You really have no control over the retirement plan marketplace. You find success in this market by responding to dynamic market conditions in a manner that your clients value and appreciate. Help yourself by writing down those areas where you believe that you could improve. What are they?

 WRITE IT
This list could include professional development, product knowledge, leadership development or industry awareness.

Q. 15 At what level of your organization will you brand?

You can choose to brand your product at any one of a number of different levels.

Your product can either be:

- You
- Your firm
- Your product
- Your delivery system
- Your broker/dealer
- Your parent company

Make a clear distinction as to how you choose to take your 401(k)/Company Retirement Plan product to the marketplace and how you will protect and preserve your brand.

Look around your office or your home and take notice of how different vendors and different suppliers choose to brand their products. For instance, household cleaning products present examples of a product being branded at the product level, the company level or even the delivery system (distribution) level.

You may be making a strategic, as well as a tactical mistake if you feel that you just sell retirement plans or sell 401(k) plans.

Q. 16 What should you create and what should you purchase?

This question should be answered with Maximum Efficiency^{SM} in mind. How will you most effectively service your client in the retirement plan industry? For example, it probably does not make sense for you to build a contact management system from scratch. What does make sense is to analyze the various database management systems available to you in the marketplace and then acquire the system that best meets your needs. Once you have purchased the database engine your next decision will be how you choose to populate the database. Here you are faced with a more realistic "create versus purchase" decision:

- Do you populate your database management system with existing contact information (i.e. business cards, letterhead, notes and past contact reports)?

or,

- Do you purchase data from one of the industry firms that specialize in data?

Simple steps for arriving at a sound decision on any of your "create versus purchase" decisions should always include:

- Comprehend the need
- Gather your data
- Study your options
- Consider "time to completion" (for each of your options)
- Analyze cost versus benefit
- Make your decision

Q. 17 How much "psychology of selling" will your sales process incorporate?

There are some sales programs that play solely on the emotions of the buyer. You need to decide if you are going to be manipulative or solution driven. Will you choose to lull the prospect into a state of perceived relief or will you educate the prospect so that they become an informed buyer who ultimately selects your service and buys your product? Do you intend to sell retirement plan services as a process for helping the plan sponsor or to deliver peace of mind to the plan sponsor concerning their participants?

Each of the sales processes requires a different approach and either can be successful.

We prefer the solution-driven approach to manipulation, but the final decision will be yours. Be cautious of the types of sales training you purchase. Many sales training firms will promote and instruct manipulative practices to generate increased sales volume. Just be sure that the training that you select employs the exact technique that you want your people to use when representing your firm.

2

Looking Forward

Many of the exercises that you complete today will have no bearing on what happens this evening or tomorrow, but many will, in some way, have an impact on what happens in a week or a month from now. Many Financial Advisors have been extraordinarily successful, but cannot tell you why or how or if that success will continue into next week or next year. More luck to them! We recognize that a certain amount of luck can have a bearing upon distinguishing a good year from a great year. But if the intent is to create a repeatable event, and string great year onto great year, then you need a certain amount of structure in your business. Doing so will stack the deck in your favor that this year and subsequent years will also be great.

Vision - Mission - Values

These are probably not new concepts to you, but applying them to your own business may be new. We find that Financial Advisors, financial organizations and businesses in general who take the time to establish a written Vision-Mission-Values Statement (VMV) and successfully communicate that VMV to their team, have a noticeably higher probability of reaching their goals. We could cite Financial Advisors or non-financial businesses as examples and provide you with copious amounts of data and testimonials, but take our word. The marketplace data supports the fact that successful companies and the better performing Financial Advisors place credence in VMV. It is difficult to have everyone working in concert in the absence of a well-conceived and effectively communicated VMV Statement.

It is possible to discuss and debate each of these concepts for a week or longer — however it is not necessary. We understand that reading this book takes you away from doing the things that you enjoy — so we are going to make this as direct and succinct as we can. For those of you who have an interest in getting immersed in the philosophical debates associated with these concepts, there is a multitude of writings on the subject and you can spend the additional time studying that if you wish.

For those who are unfamiliar with the concept, here is a brief overview of VMV:

— Vision —

The Vision is "what you want your firm, group or business to become."

The Vision describes something that is not in existence today, but something that is attainable. Another way to think of crafting the Vision is to compose a statement which answers the question, "What do you want your business to be when it grows up?" The Vision should be stated in such a manner that it can be measured, so that you know when you have reached it. Once the Vision is achieved, a new one should be established and communicated. The Vision should be established as being achievable within a three to seven year time-period. (If, for example, a company establishes a Vision that is too far into the future, say 20 years, it will be difficult to stay focused. It may seem impossible.) The Vision should be a challenge and those setting the Vision should "THINK BIG." It should not be easily achievable. Achieving the Vision should require hard work and a concerted effort to make it a reality. And remember, the Vision Statement must incorporate quantifiable and measurable components so that everyone can be made aware when success has been achieved.

A sample Vision Statement for a restaurant might be "ABC Restaurant wants to become the medium-priced restaurant of choice for residents within a seven mile radius." This can easily be measured by survey data. For a single restaurant, expansion, franchising or number of nightly diners served might also be components of the Vision Statement.

We are not in favor of revenue or profitability goals within a Vision Statement. There are multiple reasons for that, but the primary reason is that such a component may be interpreted incorrectly by employees, suppliers or customers.

Developing your Vision Statement is the initial step to redefining how you will conduct your business. Your Vision should be determined first.

— Mission —

The Mission is an extension of the Vision and answers the question "How will the Vision be achieved?"

The Mission Statement should be simple to communicate and equally simple to comprehend. You will be communicating your Mission to the public (prospects, clients, suppliers, co-workers, strategic partners etc.) For that reason, it must be simple, accurate and concise. The Mission Statement is an area where you cannot afford to be inaccurate, or stretch the truth. Keep in mind that from time to time a client or co-worker may recite the Mission Statement back to you to make a point — so be certain to establish a Mission Statement upon which you can deliver. It should never be lengthier than two sentences. If two sentences are used then they must flow logically. We have an affinity for one-sentence Mission Statements. If Fortune 500 firms can reduce what they do into one sentence, why would your business require a paragraph? We have facilitated teams where the initial Mission Statement has been over one hundred words. In each case, we were able to incorporate every concept and topic in a new, shorter version.

The Mission Statement for our sample business might be "ABC Restaurant will provide the customer with a nutritious meal, including salad, entree, two vegetables and dessert, with the entree served within 17 minutes of the order being taken, for less than $15.00."

The Mission Statement may change over time, to continually help the team accomplish the Vision, but it should not change regularly or frequently. Still, changing circumstances may require revision.

Keep in mind that the Mission Statement is a document that will be shared publicly. It should be in place for the benefit of everyone — plan sponsor, plan participants and your team. Make sure that you and your team can deliver on it.

— Values —

Values are different from the Vision and Mission in that the Values should never change. There is an acceptable level of revision and fine-tuning that occurs over time with the Vision and Mission. But the Values that one brings to a company and demonstrates through the management of the business come from the heart. For example, if "Respect" is a value of the leader of a company and thus is deemed to be a company or team Value, it is unlikely that the leader will come to the workplace and declare that "Yesterday, respect was important to me and our team. After some thought and consideration last night, I am here to tell you that we no longer value respect at this organization and from this point forward, respect of the customer and the co-worker is no longer required or tolerated." This just does not occur.

Values of our ABC Restaurant may include: Patron First, Honesty, Cleanliness and Respect

Other examples of business values are: Customer First, Integrity, Diversity, Quality, Responsibility, Teamwork and Accountability.

Values are the essence of what makes an individual who they are. It is no different at the company level. A company's Values describe what the company stands for and holds in high esteem. In most cases this exercise will be the least difficult of the three. Each of us holds some form of values near and dear to our heart. The company Values, in most cases, will not be dramatically different from the personal values we hold. Once again, they come from the heart — so there is no need to write lengthy sentences. They stand on their own as single words or, at most, three-word phrases.

The Values of your company will be shared with your clients. You should want to share them with everyone. Most leaders in business are proud of and promote their company's Values.

We prefer to see anywhere from three to eight Values for any Financial Advisor team. Some have a shopping list for every situation. Three is better than twenty. Your entire team must be aware of the Values by which you operate.

Now is the time to have pen in hand. We'll begin with some macro level questions for you or the leadership group of your team.

Q. 18 What is your team Vision?

(By writing the answers to the following four questions, you should know if you have a clear Vision.)
- What do you want to accomplish?
- What do you want the team to have accomplished in five years time?
- Where are you taking your team?
- Does the Vision you have described define what you wish the team to become?

 WRITE IT

Is the Vision a "stretch" for you and/or your team? (It should be.)

Does the Vision accurately represent what you intend your company to be in the near future?

Is the Vision you have described a measurable event? (It must be.)

If the answer to any of the prior three questions is "no" then retool the Vision until the answer is "yes" to all three questions.

Q. 19 What is your team Mission?

- How will you achieve your reputation?
- How will you and/or your team make the Vision a reality?
- Why will a prospect choose your expertise and your firm over another firm?
- What day-to-day activities will make you better than the competition?

 WRITE IT

Is the Mission easy for you to describe?

Is it easy for your team to comprehend and communicate to others?

Is it concise?

Is it simple for the client to comprehend?

If the answer to any of these four questions is "no," then you must re-state it. You may have all the vital components, but it may need to be re-crafted so that the answer to all four is "yes."

Q. 20 What are your team Values?

- What do you feel is important?
- What qualities do you hold in high regard?
- What can your client be confident of when conducting business with you?
- How will the client be treated by your team?

 WRITE IT

Is what you have written, as Values, truly important to you?

Does it represent what you and your company will commit to?

Is there zero tolerance for anything less than upholding the Values?

Is each of the Values listed by using no more than three words?

Does your list include at least three and no more than eight Values?

Are your team's Values clearly stated and unambiguous?

If these six questions have any "no" answers, you may need to re-think your Values. You want to answer all of these with a resounding "yes!" You may need to reduce the number or clarify them. Your Values underpin how your business operates. You are building the foundation of your business in this exercise. Be clear.

Q. 21 *What is the appropriate process for establishing the Vision statement?*

The visioning session can assume many forms. We will address three Visioning processes that we know to be successful.

The Napkin Approach — In this process one person (Financial Advisor or the leader of a team) possesses a crystal-clear understanding of "where I need to take this place." The napkin form does not leave a door open for outside ideas or input — because the leader employs an autocratic style that works. (We call this the napkin approach in reference to the many contracts, plans and models that have been penned on such. In many cases, the ideas are so clear and concise that they fit on a napkin.) Although there are limitations to this style, it can be extraordinarily effective for many leaders in the right environment. The napkin approach does omit some of the exercises that foster teamwork within a group, but it has proven to be a successful style if conducted in the right environment by a capable leader. The style is short on outside ideas and camaraderie. There have been many worthwhile documents penned on a napkin. Although it does not work for most teams, we recognize the effectiveness of this style by a capable leader. For some individual Financial Advisors the napkin approach may be appropriate, but we suggest a follow-up transfer of the information to a more traditional document. It just looks more professional!

Internal Facilitation — The internal facilitation process of establishing a Vision is used by most Financial Advisors. The process can be very effective for the experienced team who is fortunate enough to have a skilled facilitator on their team. A good facilitator will stimulate the thought process of everyone in the group. But you should be aware of the challenges associated with using an internal facilitator, and there are a few.

First and foremost, facilitators from your own team or group will always be considered "insiders," which could stymie open and honest discussion. Sometimes people in the group can be intimidated or feel shot down when an internal facilitator makes the exact same observation that an external facilitator might make. There can also be reluctance to share among the team because of the fear of "saying something stupid." In a corporate environment, the same fear factor is present but there may be an added concern of: "will someone else pass my good ideas to everybody else in the firm and take credit for them?" Although we have outlined some of the drawbacks, if you have the appropriate skills available to you within your firm we feel that you should attempt to utilize them. You can always re-think the decision if the session is not productive for you and your team.

External Facilitation — External facilitators are used most often by teams that want to make a major and immediate impact on their business in the shortest amount of time possible. The external facilitator is a skilled professional who is comfortable with the process and function of facilitation. There is no "ax to grind" or preconceived notions when someone from outside comes to the table. The team usually benefits from the outside influence by gaining a new perspective on the business. It is usually a valuable experience for all. The drawback to utilizing an outside facilitator is that they will be more expensive than either the internal facilitator or the napkin approach. In managing your business you should employ a cost-benefit analysis to determine where you will receive the most value. The external facilitator should provide your team with advance materials so the session time is most productive.

All three styles of establishing your Vision can work, however, for best results, we recommend utilizing an outside facilitator for this exercise.

Q. 22 *What is the best way to begin a session for developing our Vision-Mission-Values?*

Begin with an open, honest discussion. Permit the session to progress naturally. Let it flow. Encourage everyone to contribute. Allow team members to say exactly what is on their minds. (Within reason, that is. In groups, one person can go on for what seems to be an eternity. Do not permit one individual or thought to monopolize your session.)

Q. 23 *What key questions should I ask in order to develop my organizational (or team) Vision, Mission and Values?*

- What would your clients say about you?
- What would your clients say about your team?
- What Values would your clients use to describe you?
- What Values would your clients use to describe your team?
- What Values guide your actions?
- What Values do you want to guide your actions?

Q. 24 *Where should I focus my efforts?*

First consider what your firm structure permits you to deliver. Clearly understand the structure and your leeway within it, then develop your individual strength, be it consultative, client first, niche, transaction based, education based or something else.

 WRITE IT

Q. 25 **Do you (or your team) have biases?**

Certain biases are more or less built into various compensation schemes. If biases exist, can you exploit them for the benefit of the team? Consider your brand (again, that's YOU!). You are the focus, and you are the product of skills, biases, beliefs, aspirations, desires. The more you know about you, the sharper the focus and the more effectively you can communicate with your team. This will enhance the overall probability of achieving your Vision.

Q. 26 **When asked by a plan sponsor to explain why you (your team) should be considered to service their company retirement savings plan, how would you respond?**

You must have a strong response to this question. It does not need to be long, but it does need to be strong!

> **Example:** *"We are positioned to serve 401(k)/Company Retirement Plans in the manufacturing segment of industry by delivering unbiased advice to employers and employees. We do that while assisting you, the plan sponsor, in the management of your fiduciary responsibility and helping you to avoid the fiduciary pitfalls. Our team also comprehends the tax challenges facing your executive team." (But only say what is accurate and true!)*

 WRITE IT

Q. 27 *What should I do if the response from our team is not consistent?*

When all team members deliver the same response you can be assured that all share the same Vision, Mission and Values — all have the same "focus of purpose." Everyone is "pointed in the same direction" and you and your team are well on your way toward success! And of course the opposite is true, if all team members cannot recite the same "verse," then you have some work to do in clarifying and communicating to the team the correct response.

3

Your
Strategic Plan

Your Strategic Plan is a written document in which you define the near- and long-term strategy of the organization. The Strategic Plan should describe the key challenges that must be overcome in order to make your Vision a reality. The Strategic Plan is a "big-picture" view of what will take you to the Vision. You will notice the Strategic Plan does not include the tasks or activities but only the overarching concepts. Activities and initiatives are specified in the Business Plan (described in detail in the following chapter).

Financial Advisors are faced with many strategic planning decisions. A prime example is whether to operate as a Registered Investment Financial Advisor (fee-only) or as a Registered Representative (commission). This is a "big picture" decision that will have a major impact on how you run your business. For instance, if you are approaching the retirement plan market as a commissioned Financial Advisor, it is likely that you have access to additional investment services and products to offer your clients. If you are approaching the market as a fee-only Financial Advisor, then you may be limited or possibly excluded from offering any additional individual or institutional investment services.

As a commissioned sales person you have to make a decision as to whether you will embark on cross-selling the plan sponsor organization and individual plan participants or not. Once you have made the decision to utilize cross-selling, inform the decision maker early-on of your ability and capabilities. There is no better defense against your "direct sold" or "fee only" competitors than a good offense and proactively informing the decision makers about your full capabilities. When informed by your "direct sold" or "fee only" competitors that you will attempt to cross-sell the company and plan participants, the best response you can hope for from the decision maker to the "informant" is, "Yes, I know. They fully explained their capabilities to us already."

Now for the "fee only" Financial Advisors, be prepared when the decision maker turns to you and asks, "What else can you do for me and my organization?" Your service menu could contain investment performance monitoring, investment policy development, employee surveying and/or employee communication campaign development. You should be ready to tout these services and the associated benefits if asked.

As you can see, the Strategic decision (fee-only or commission) comes first. Everything else — how you approach your prospects, what specific products you will offer, etc. — will be dependent upon that decision.

Q. 28 *What is a Strategic Plan?*

Your Strategic Plan is the list of major initiatives which, when accomplished, will enable you to achieve your personal or team Vision.

Strategic Plan ➤ Vision

Q. 29 *Do I need a Strategic Plan?*

Everyone needs a Strategic Plan if they expect to have a positive impact on their current situation. Different outcomes result from changed behavior. The Strategic Plan is one way to outline where behavioral change is required.

> **Example:** *Perhaps your current information management system is incapable of adequately supporting your efforts to realize your Vision. That can be identified within the Strategic Plan as a major initiative. The specific steps for improving your information management system would be detailed within the Business Plan. The headings for these activities might be 1) determine a project leader, 2) analyze available options, 3) create a short list, 4) check references and 5) make the selection.*

This takes you to the point of having made a selection and you would conduct similar steps during the implementation and data transfer phases.

Q. 30 *How do I begin to develop a Strategic Plan?*

The concepts from Chapters 1 and 2 and the answers to the questions listed there should provide you with sufficient background and direction for the development of your Strategic Plan. The work you have conducted on Vision-Mission-Values will serve as your Strategic Plan's foundation. Simply put, what will it take to accomplish your Vision? You may not have a full view of each of the individual components, but you should have a good idea of where you want your business to focus. The Vision is your ultimate destination, and the Strategic Plan serves as your North Star in guiding you to that destination.

Q. 31 *How do I make sure that my Strategic Plan is the correct one for my team?*

Do not get bogged-down with the details of a Strategic Plan at this early stage. Implement it as soon as possible to avoid "paralysis by analysis." If you find that certain components of the Strategic Plan do not contribute to achieving your Vision, then stop pursuing them and re-focus your efforts elsewhere.

Q. 32 *How often should I revisit and revise my Strategic Plan?*

Ideally, you should review your Strategic Plan once every year. Until you feel confident that you are on the right course we suggest reviewing the document at least quarterly to confirm the focus.

Q. 33 *What should my Strategic Plan include?*

You must include those steps that will take you to the full achievement of your Vision. The Strategic Plan is your Vision analyzed and dissected into work-related activities, concepts, or process improvements. Strategic planning activities should be separated into two main categories — those objectives to attain in less than one year and those objectives to attain in more than one year.

Q. 34 *How will my Strategic Plan be developed?*

You can choose to develop your own Strategic Plan internally or you can utilize an outside resource. If you have never gone down this path before, you would greatly benefit by having someone experienced in the creation of Strategic Plans assist you with this process. Generally, if you are a team (more than one producer) you should include your most senior members in this process. If you are an individual Financial Advisor, you will be crafting your plan on your own. In either case, if this is your first attempt at the plan, utilizing outside resources will save you considerable time and a substantial amount of money.

Q. 35 *How do I prioritize major initiatives within my Strategic Plan?*

This can be a daunting task for the rookie strategic planner. The interesting part is that prioritizing becomes much simpler during the course of business once the Strategic Plan is put in place. The plan must have a logical flow from a micro standpoint, and as it relates to work productivity. If your tasks include building a database and making cold calls, you would never begin your cold calling efforts prior to obtaining your calling database, loading your calling database and working your database. We emphasize logical workflow and work processes that build upon each other to continually move you toward Maximum Efficiency.

Q. 36 *What do I need to accomplish and by when?*

Keeping an eye on your Vision, decide what you will accomplish in 30/60/90/180/360 days and beyond.

Defining specific activities and production objectives within specific timeframes allows you to establish a series of achievable outcomes that will lead you to your longer term goals. Assess the applicability and production objective of each activity and then allocate sufficient time to achieve each goal.

Q. 37 *How do I determine the priority of tasks?*

Certain tasks will logically need to precede others.

> **Example:** *In business development, "cleansing" your database should take place prior to embarking on a direct mail campaign. Consider the case in which a direct mail campaign is to occur during a 120 day period. Logically you will want to build some of the pieces*

prior to beginning the campaign. It would be most beneficial to scrub or clean the database prior to initiating any mail-drop. Not doing so would be a waste of time, postage, stationery and internal and/or external resources. (This example may sound elementary, but we have heard producers say, "It is easier for me to just mail everyone, than it is to scrub and update the database." That may be a true statement – but it is an incredible waste of time, material and money.)

Q. 38 *Is my Strategic Plan the same as my Business Plan?*

No. The Business Plan will be covered in depth in the next chapter. Strategy must be decided before the development of a Business Plan can begin.

4

Your
Business Plan

In contrast to your Strategic Plan, your Business Plan will outline the activities and initiatives that you will use to achieve those outcomes outlined within your Strategic Plan. It takes the intended outcomes from your "big picture" strategy and distills them into workable actions or specific initiatives. We emphasize that the Business Plan should always support your Strategic Plan. All activities from this point forward should satisfy the goal of fully supporting your Strategic Plan.

A Business Plan describes and builds the tasks and outlines the accomplishments necessary to achieve your Strategic Plan. Doing so will ultimately result in you and your team achieving the Vision.

Business Plan ➤ Strategic Plan ➤ Vision

The Business Plan should provide direction for all of the activities associated with your initiatives as outlined in your Strategic Plan.

As we have previously noted, 401(k)/Company Retirement Plan business development is a time-consuming, labor-intensive process. It could take up to a year from the time you first contact an employer until the time you receive your initial compensation. If you have a clear picture of what you are trying to accomplish along your sales journey, you can best structure your time and effort.

A Business Plan helps you to focus. You will likely have a limited amount of time to spend in pursuing the sale during the long gestation period associated with acquiring a 401(k)/Company Retirement Plan.

A Business Plan helps you to focus on the immediate tasks at hand. It identifies obstacles and serves as a roadmap for reaching your near-term objectives; it supports your Strategic Plan, which in turn leads you to your Vision.

The 401(k)/Company Retirement Plan Business Plan that we discuss should be a key part of your total Business Plan. If your overall business does not operate with a Business Plan, then the components we use to describe the 401(k)/Company Retirement Plan Business Plan can certainly be used as a template for strategically positioning your overall business.

There may be successful Financial Advisors who have never written nor even read a Business Plan. However, they should each consider the following:

- How much better could results have been had they been executing a thoughtfully devised Business Plan instead of randomly storing ideas and objectives only in their head?
- How much time could they have saved, or spent with their family, by having a written Business Plan to guide their activities?
- How much more successful could their team associates have been and how much more would everyone have learned by participating in the process of developing a Business Plan?
- And, with the appropriate guidance as is often detailed within a Business Plan, where might the team be today?

We have one or two quick questions for you:

Q. 39 Do you have an "old" plan?

If the answer to this question is "no," then go directly to the Business Plan Overview.

If the answer to this question is "yes"…

Q. 40 What does your "old" Business Plan look like?

Bring it out for review while building your new Business Plan. We suggest that you keep it close at hand to compare how many of the components that we outline are included in your existing Business Plan. This will help you determine if you would be better served by starting from scratch or if you have the luxury of just tweaking your existing plan and filling in any missing categories or components.

Business Plan Overview

The Business Plan is your team's guide to success. It will always support the Vision-Mission-Values of the team as well as those of the overall organization. The Business Plan will also support the Strategic Plan. Create a well-defined and structured Business Plan for your 401(k)/Company Retirement Plan business. To follow is an example of the major categories and components used in many successful Business Plans.

Major Categories
A. Operational
B. Marketing
C. Service
D. Compliance

Components
- Business Development
- Client Retention Activities
- Communication Strategy
- Database Management
- Goals
- Measurement
- Presentation Management
- Product Champion
- Professional Development
- Roles & Responsibilities
- Service Agreement
- Target Market
- The Business Structure

Some of the these components will be covered here, but others are of the magnitude that they require their own chapter. As we progress through the Business Plan we will be inserting each of the above components into one of the first three major categories (Operations, Marketing and Service.)

You will notice that the fourth major category is Compliance. Compliance is its own category due to the unique compliance requirements within each firm. Your activities, processes, and systems are all mandated to satisfy the requirements of your internal compliance as well as the guidelines established by the appropriate regulatory agencies that oversee you and your business practices.

It is not necessary for your Business Plan to be an exact one-for-one match of what is outlined here. It is more important that the major initiatives of your firm have been identified in the Strategic Plan and that components to support those initiatives are incorporated into the Business Plan. Always remember that the Business Plan is derived from the Strategic Plan and that both must support your efforts to reach your Vision.

You should examine every task you perform in your business and ask yourself, "Does this task or activity help the team achieve either the Strategic Plan or the Vision?" (You will see variations of this question being asked throughout this book. Its importance bears repeating.) If what you are doing does not fit into the strategic focus of the organization or does not help you to accomplish your strategic initiatives, then there is no reason to include it in the Business Plan and there is simply no reason to perform the task. (We realize that there are always exceptions. However the number of exceptions that you accommodate within your business will have a direct impact on the level of efficiency that you and your team are able to achieve. Exception processing is inefficient and costly!)

We have reformulated and prioritized the components of a typical Business Plan and inserted them into the respective major categories. Business Plan components should look something like this:

A. Operational
- The Business Structure
- Goals
- Roles and Responsibilities
- Communication Strategy
- Database Management
- Measurement

B. Marketing
- Service Agreement
- Target Market
- Business Development
- Presentation Management
- Professional Development

C. Service
- Product Champion
- Client Retention Activities
- Service Agreement

D. Compliance

If you are beginning this process from scratch (meaning that you have just created your Vision-Mission-Values and your Strategic Plan) then we suggest a logical order of progression. You will notice that some of the components of building your successful business could fall under different major categories. We will use this order for the purpose of this text but please be aware that your specific situation may require a different order due to your unique set of circumstances or priorities. Your priorities may be different and we recognize that. When starting from scratch, this list can serve as a guideline.

You will notice that the Service Agreement appears in two major categories. We will explain why at a later point in this chapter.

Components Used To Build Your Business Plan

— A. Operational —

The Business Structure

Q. 41 *What are the possible structures for my business?*

There are primarily three options for non-W-2 employee business. These structures can be any of the following:

- Corporation
- Limited Liability (Corporation or Partnership)
- DBA (Doing Business As)

(The business structure of a W-2 employee is defined by virtue of the employee/employer relationship. The W-2 employee assumes the formal business registration of the parent company in most cases.)

Q. 42 *Which of these structures is correct for my business?*

There are few questions in this book for which we refer you to other sources — this is one of them. Even though we have an understanding of the different business structures and have operated businesses within and through each of these structures, the very best advice we can provide here is to direct you to speak with an attorney who is also a CPA. A CPA can best describe the tax consequences of the different structures whereas the attorney can best describe the legal ramifications of each business structure. By speaking with an attorney who is also a CPA you can keep from feeling like a tennis ball as you might when you are seeking advice from two different professionals. If your situation dictates that you must seek the opinion of two separate individuals (CPA and an attorney), our recommendation is to have them both be present at the same meeting so that by the end of that meeting you will have resolved the business structure decision.

You should come prepared to that meeting with a list of questions and an agenda. Keep all parties on schedule with the agenda. This will surely be an expensive meeting—make the most of your time and money.

Goals

Goals are intended outcomes, derived from the strategic initiatives that support the Vision.

Analyzing your territory, situation and opportunity assists you in confirming the viability of your goals. If you live in a rural isolated area and your goal is to bring in $200 million in 401(k) assets, you may have to expand your prospecting efforts to incorporate geography that encompasses a sufficient "inventory" of 401(k)/Company Retirement Plan opportunities. Your goals must be based upon reasonable assumptions. Confirming your business opportunity and potential are the outcomes of your analysis. You will be able to set realistic goals as a result of your work.

Q. 43 What are your personal goals?

Be as specific with your personal goals as you are with your professional goals. All goals need a map or a plan. You may also require tools in order to succeed. Is a personal goal for you the purchase of a primary or vacation home? Do you have a "life" outside your professional world? What do you want to do when you are not "at work"? It is beneficial to have a handle on your personal goals when you are developing your overall marketing strategy. What is important to you will determine which segment of the market you participate in. Your personal goals may not drive your position in the marketplace, however you will want the marketplace you enter to be consistent with your chosen lifestyle. For example: If you have three small children and you want to be home every night to watch them grow during their younger years, you would not be happy participating in the jumbo market sales where 75 percent of your time or greater is spent on the road. In this personal scenario, you are better served by satisfying a need in a more local market — where you can sleep in your own bed every night.

 WRITE IT

Q. 44 Do you have written goals?

Be extra careful when you answer this question. This question is calling for a one-word "yes or no" response.

If your goals (any of them) are only "in your head," then the answer to this question is "no"!

If some are written and some are not, the answer is "no"!

If you answered "yes," congratulations! You are one of a microscopic subset within your industry.

Q. 45 Could you verbally state your goals, right now, without reviewing them?

If you cannot state your goals right now, without reviewing them, then the answer to this question is simple. "No"!

Q. 46 *Why do I need to establish goals?*

You established the need for goals when you wrote your Strategic Plan. Goals provide measures for the accomplishment of your Strategic Plan.

Goals are measurable events or processes which, when accomplished, will ensure the likelihood that you will achieve your strategic objectives.

If you are working to accomplish a goal then you must keep your eye on the intended outcome. A football analogy is an excellent example; the team always knows what the goal is, as well as the location of the goal. You need to constantly know what your goals are and the distance between you and your goals.

Q. 47 *How do I establish my goals?*

After breaking down the Vision in your Strategic Plan you will need to distill the Strategic Plan into specific objectives and major initiatives. This occurs in your Business Plan. Your goals become those measures, which, when accomplished, will make your Business Plan a success.

Business Plan ➤ Goals ➤ Strategic Plan ➤ Vision

Continuing with the football analogy, here is a way to illustrate this concept:

Football Team		Your Business
Cross the goal line of opponent every time you possess the ball	**Business Plan**	Close 5% of new appointments
Win every season game	**Goal**	Five new appointments per week
Win every playoff game	**Strategic Plan**	Increase annual fees 20%
Superbowl Champions	**Vision**	Retire "comfortably" in ten years

Roles and Responsibilities

If you are a lone producer, then determining roles and responsibilities is rather simple — you are destined to do it all!

Q. 48 Are you a lone producer with an administrative assistant?

If you are working with an administrative assistant you need to determine which tasks you will keep and which tasks you should assign to your assistant. The two biggest mistakes made by individual Financial Advisors who have an administrative assistant are:

- Failing to provide ongoing coaching to the assistant
- Not clearly communicating expectations

These may sound like similar challenges. However one has to do with long-term expectations while the other addresses ongoing coaching and guidance.

No one can know what you are thinking unless you tell them. It is never safe to assume that someone will act in any manner that you desire or that they will complete a task as you desire, unless you provide the direction. In many cases an administrative assistant could deliver substantially more value and provide increased efficiencies to the producer if only the assistant were directed properly. This occurs because either the producer does not have the skills to coach the assistant or the producer feels that no one can perform as well as they!

If you have a weak administrative assistant, you need to replace them. You and your business are destined to stay at a low level of production when you are strapped with an inefficient or a weak administrative assistant

You must still consider yourself a leader even though your team consists of only you and your administrative assistant.

Q. 49 Are you the leader of a production team?

If you are the leader of the team, your primary consideration should be to lead. Then and only then (after you have carried out your leadership responsibilities) may you take on other roles such as producer, business developer or any other. Production needs to be secondary to your leadership role. Everything needs to be secondary to the leadership role. We have devoted Chapter 14 to the topic of leadership.

Q. 50 Are each of your team members aware of their respective roles and responsibilities?

It is your responsibility as leader of your team to ensure that each team member is fully aware of their area of responsibility. Specific areas of responsibility should be communicated to everyone in writing so that each member of the team has accountability to the group.

Q. 51 *What is the difference between roles and responsibilities?*

A team member's role will be defined as an area of oversight. It may be accounting, compliance, production, investments, education or possibly another area.

Responsibilities will encompass the specific tasks that the team expects to be performed by the individuals placed in specific roles.

An individual's role could be business development. In that role their responsibilities may be to manage the database, establish a calling program, set appointments for producers and update the database upon completion of the appointment.

The role is general; the associated responsibilities are specific.

Q. 52 *Why should the roles of my team members be in writing?*

Documenting the roles of all team members benefits each individual member as well as the entire team. It will serve to establish expectations.

We are not talking about a lengthy document that outlines every specific task. Documenting a team member's role should be completed within two to five sentences. This should not be a monumental task nor should it take more than 20 minutes of your time to define the role of each team member.

Q. 53 *What are responsibilities?*

Responsibilities are the tasks and processes that a team member in a specific role will accomplish on a regular basis. Responsibilities should be explicitly defined so that there is always an understanding of the intended outcome. This provides clear and unambiguous direction concerning what is expected and who is accountable.

It is your duty as the leader of your team to ensure that each member is fully aware of their specific responsibilities as they relate to team performance. Responsibilities create accountability.

Example:
The Role might be Administrative Assistant…
The Responsibilities may include:
- *Answering the telephone*
- *Preparing proposals*
- *Preparing meeting agendas, etc.*

Q. 54 *What is the best way to determine which team member should be responsible for performing specific tasks?*

Start by asking team members their preference. Observe team members in their roles and decide whether to retain or remove them from the role. This decision should be based on your best judgment of their ability to manage their assigned responsibilities. There are administrative tasks and there are those that only you can execute. Your team will operate most efficiently by having the very best individuals occupy positions in which they can succeed and feel good about their accomplishments. A crucial question is, "Are you willing to delegate tasks which you know you should not be performing?" It is important that you build your team with a mix of complimentary professionals who share your Vision-Mission-Values and you must be willing to utilize them. No one can do it all. You must be willing to delegate tasks in order for your team to be successful.

Communicating Strategy

Q. 55 *How do I insure that all team members understand their next step in the plan?*

This is a case where a little bit of communication can go a long way in improving morale, productivity and profitability. Excluding the leadership team, a frequent complaint among the rest of the team members is that they do not know what is occurring within the team on a day-to-day basis. That complaint frequently surfaces among Financial Advisor teams. Do not assume that because you can see the big picture and understand what everyone should be doing, that all team members automatically know what to do next. Communicate your expectations on a regular basis. Hold regularly scheduled meetings for the benefit of the entire team. The general purpose of these meetings is to keep everyone rowing in the same direction.

Q. 56 Do you have regularly scheduled meetings with the purpose of keeping everyone in the group informed?

If the answer to this question is "no," then you must change your attitude and behavior towards communicating with the group.

We suggest that you institute regular weekly meetings in order to keep everyone focused on team goals and objectives. The team should always be aware of where it stands relative to meeting team goals.

Q. 57 *Should there be an agenda for the regularly scheduled meeting?*

Yes! Meetings without an agenda generally tend to be a waste of time. The best way to have team members look forward to your meeting is by adhering to a prepared agenda. The agenda must include a starting time and a "worst case" ending time. Be respectful of your team members' working hours so that they can efficiently plan their day.

Q. 58 *How do I make sure that each of the specific agenda topics is covered?*

It is wise to have each of your team members be responsible for a specific category on the agenda.

Always include a heading for Compliance on the agenda of any regularly scheduled meeting.

Q. 59 *What is the best way to insure that every team member shares the same focus?*

Scheduling and holding team meetings with a prepared agenda and allowing every team member to play a part in the meeting will foster teamwork and will promote a shared focus on the achievement of activities and goals.

Database Management

Since database management is one of the top three areas where Financial Advisors falter, we will spend a considerable amount of time helping you to get your database working for you instead of against you. There are two components to database management. The database is the collection of prospects with the corresponding relevant data. The contact management system is a software program used to organize and manipulate the data or a subset of the data.

Q. 60 How well do you currently manage prospect data?

This is a broad, open-ended question. Your response to this question will provide an indication of where there may be substantial room for improvement. To easily answer this question we will offer you three possible answers: A) poorly, B) so-so, or C) very well.

If your response is C , then we suggest that you move directly to the next section on Measurement. If your response is not C, continue on.

Q. 61 *What database options are available to me?*

There are many different options available to you for the collection and acquisition of customer contact data. You should check with your manager, others in your firm, your parent company and the database firms directly. Almost all Financial Advisors have access to some form of database with their existing relationships. If you do not have access to a database by virtue of your existing relationships you must consider purchasing data. The following web sites can help:

www.401kexchange.com
www.larkspurdata.com
http://www.jda@freeerisa.com/

If you value and respect your time, you will choose to work from a database.

Q. 62 *What contact management system options are available to me?*

To effectively manage your leads, activity and time, a contact management program must be in place. The system that you select should be flexible, expandable and relatively simple to operate. You will use the contact management system for keeping notes and tracking your progress with prospects and clients. It is possible that you are handcuffed with the requirement of working exclusively with a corporate contact management system. If that is the case, then take the time to understand the features and functionality of that internal system as well as its limitations. Understanding the limitations of the corporate system is equally as important as understanding its features. Where limitations exist, you need to find some workable solution that will put you, at the very least, on par with the state-of-the-art systems that a segment of your competition is using.

There are too many options in the contact management arena to begin citing examples. Again, we suggest that you speak with others in your firm to find the best solution for you.

Q. 63 *Is a contact management program really necessary?*

Absolutely! Contact management software has given each of us the opportunity to be substantially more productive than we would be otherwise. We all have the same capability to be much more productive as the result of such systems or tools. A big factor in how productive and successful you will become is related to the extent to which you embrace technology and utilize information management software capabilities.

Q. 64 *What should I be looking for in a contact management program?*

At a bare minimum, you will need a contact management program that can efficiently track prospects, clients, paper, dates and future events. If you are on a network you should learn your internal requirements as it relates to multi-seat users and the sharing of information.

Additional features that others may want to see within your program include: record-keeping/retention, expense reports and project management. Although these features are not your primary concern in a contact management program, they may be helpful to you from the standpoint of time and productivity management.

You should always consider the possibility of future enhancements to the software, but never let anything take precedence over your need for basic functionality and efficiency. It is possible that you may need to upgrade your computer system in order to satisfy the hardware requirements of the software that you select.

The efficient use of your time will help you to achieve the goals of the organization. There is no better time saver in a Financial Advisor business than a properly selected and efficiently run database management tool.

Q. 65 *How do I develop my database of prospects?*

Begin the development of your database by accurately "mining " the data within your current book or client list. You will also augment your database by asking your professional and social contacts for names. The number of 401(k)/Company Retirement Plans prospects in your database should be large enough to result in your achieving your new plan growth requirements based on conservative closing assumptions. A good rule of thumb is the "10% rule." If you want to have $200 million in new 401(k)/Company Retirement Plan assets within 10 years and you project the average asset plan to be $10 million, then you need 20 plans. Conservatively you may need 200 "cold" prospects, based on 40% (80) becoming "warm" prospects and 50% of those (40) becoming "hot" prospects and finally 50% of those (20) becoming clients. (See Appendix B for more detail on this example.)

Q. 66 *How should I proceed if I am new to the analysis of database and contact management software?*

We suggest that you speak with others in the industry that may have been down this road before. If that approach does not yield a workable solution for you, here are some other areas you can consider:

- If you are interested in investing in such a program for the first time or looking to upgrade we suggest you make a trip to www.ehow.com.

- Check reviews in computer magazines and on the Internet to help you narrow your choices.
- Download demo versions from the manufacturers' web sites to try specific programs.
- Try the information manager included in your office suite program if you already have Corel WordPerfect Suite, Lotus SmartSuite or Microsoft Office.
- Conduct an internet search on the terms "contact management software" or "database software."

Things to keep in mind when looking at different systems:

- Decide whether you need a basic or professional (also called a "relational") program. Relational programs allow you to link many separate databases together, providing you with the ability to "query."
- Look for compatibility with your wireless organizer if you have one.
- Make sure the program has network features if you need them.
- Compare ease-of-use features such as phone and address book, appointment book and contact management.
- Compare time and date tracking capabilities, such as calendar or planner features, as well as sharing and managing schedules across a network, to-do lists, and schedule tracking and display.
- Compare customizable screen views.
- Compare record-keeping capabilities for information management, expense reports and project management.
- Determine integration possibilities with other applications.
- Consider mail management tools, such as e-mail features and mail merge.
- Compare the file sizes of applications if you plan to use your personal information manager on a laptop computer.
- Make sure your computer meets the system requirements of any program you download or buy.

Q. 67 *What client/prospect data should be maintained within my system?*

Everyone has a different view on what the ideal database should contain. We suggest the following data fields:

- Company name
- Address
- Company phone number
- Company web site address
- Fax number
- Notes (free form — for call report type information)
- Last contact date
- Next step
- Next contact date

- Primary contact name
- Primary contact phone number
- Primary contact e-mail address

- Decision maker name
- Decision maker phone number
- Decision maker e-mail address

- Retirement committee members
- Investment committee members
- Next review date

- Total value of the plan
- Current program provider 1
- Current program provider 2
- Education provider
- Recordkeeper

- Average participant account balance
- Annual contributions to the plan
- Total number of employees
- Total number of plan participants

- Location(s) (if other than the headquarters)
- Type of industry
- Average tenure for employees
- Number of company locations

Q. 68 *Who should be responsible for entering data into the database?*

The question here is one of centralization versus decentralization. There is no single correct answer. Some groups or teams will find it efficient and ultimately more effective to have one individual manage the data. If that is the case, everyone on the team needs to be aware that the database manager will be protective of the data. Having one database manager is a bit more cumbersome at the point of data entry, but you will enjoy the benefits of a clean and accurate database. Having one person manage the data also centralizes report production, direct mail generation and any administrative functions.

You may choose to have each individual enter their own data for clients and prospects. This may save time, but the trade-off is that the quality and integrity of the data may be compromised due to the varying degrees of sophistication (and typing skills) among those who enter it. Perhaps you will choose to have a form that is completed and then submitted to an assistant for entry into the database.

It is impossible to describe the best data management process for everyone. This is where the "art" of managing your business comes to the fore. Whichever process you finally select, it will have a lasting impact on the growth of your business. You should make it the standard for your organization. An assessment of your own internal capabilities and resources should help you determine who is best positioned to manage your list of database prospects.

You do have a database of prospects, don't you? There are plenty of proven 401(k)/Company Retirement Plan Financial Advisors and producers who do not have an adequate database of prospects or system to track clients. This severely limits their potential for future growth. While databases can be intimidating if you are new to them, they are powerful tools for managing information and processes and are indispensable to your business.

Your database grows more valuable with time only if you continually populate your database with new and updated data.

Measurement

By measuring the performance of key areas of your business you will collect data. The analysis of this data transforms it into information that you can use to discover which processes, systems and/or behaviors need to be modified in order to show improvement.

We will address some quick questions here, however we have devoted Chapter 18 entirely to the subject of measurement.

Q. 69 *How can I measure my progress?*

You have to be able to assess your progress in accomplishing your tasks. We are proponents of measuring the key components of managing your business. The areas where you may have failed are just as important as your successes — maybe more. We utilize what we refer to as Primary Measurement Points (PMPs) for monitoring performance targets. PMPs are defined for both your acquisition and retention activities, and serve as both a beacon and a guardrail to keep you and your business on track toward your goals. (See Chapter 18 for more on Primary Measurement Points.)

Q. 70 *How do I utilize the information gathered through measurement?*

Take the information resulting from measurement and assess it with the specific activity or initiative that generated the information. Did the measurement exceed, meet or not meet the expectations that you had for that activity or initiative? If the results of your measurement are not satisfactory, then make the changes necessary to accomplish your goal for the activity and initiative.

— B. Marketing —

Your marketing plan describes how you will promote your business, develop your prospects, transform them into clients and retain them with extraordinary service. It describes how you will communicate and deliver your value proposition during both the acquisition and retention phases of your business. It will serve as a step-by-step action plan in your pursuit of the 401(k)/Company Retirement Plan market. This is your plan for success and no one else has more responsibility for your success than you. It is not your prospects' responsibility to become your clients. It may be their privilege, but it is not their responsibility! And it is not their responsibility to stay as your clients.

It is your responsibility to profile, inform and present to your prospects. It is your responsibility to discover and develop, with the assistance of your clients, appropriate service strategies. So how will you inform your prospects of your capabilities?

Service Agreement

The Service Agreement is described and illustrated in more detail in Appendix A.

Q. 71 *Why is the Service Agreement in both major categories of Marketing and Service?*

Your Service Agreement will distinguish you from the competition. It also sends a message to the industry that you are serious about caring for your client.

When properly constructed, the Service Agreement serves as such a powerful management tool for both you and your client that communicating its availability to prospects could be to your competitive advantage.

Q. 72 *Can you describe a successful Service Agreement?*

The successful Service Agreement will be a collective understanding between the Financial Advisor and the 401(k)/Company Retirement Plan executives. Each organization will have its own version of a Service Agreement. It is less formal than an Operating Agreement. It should clearly delineate responsibilities and inspire confidence among all involved parties. A comprehensive Service Agreement will properly set expectations, define deliverables and hold respective parties accountable for performance.

Target Market

You defined in your Business Plan your target market, describing the type of industry, size of employee base, average employee compensation, proximity to your office and/or home and other parameters. Now you will define how to identify and reach out to these prospects and how to remain in contact with them once they have become clients.

Q. 73 *How do I determine the type of prospects and clients I should be working with?*

Let's get introspective! Who are you working with currently? If you do not currently have any 401(k)/Company Retirement Plans, prepare a list of current individual clients or social contacts that could refer you to their company plan or other 401(k)/Company Retirement Plan plans in your target market.

If you have 401(k)/Company Retirement Plans, prepare an inventory of your current employer-sponsored savings plan business including the following information:

- Name of company
- Type of plan (401(k), defined benefit, profit sharing, etc.)
- Year acquired
- Industry
- Total plan assets
- Number of eligible employees
- Number of participants
- Proximity

Q. 74 *What is the definition of a target prospect?*

By merging existing account and prospect information with your realistic "wish list" of prospect plans you will begin to construct a clear picture of your target prospect (or sweet spot.) Include industry type, number of employees (as a range, for instance 100 – 200), plan assets, physical locations — just to name a few characteristics.

Q. 75 What segment of the market is your "sweet spot"?

Asked another way, what is the segment of the 401(k)/Company Retirement Plan business that you desire most? If given a choice, what business do you want? Keep in mind your Vision and what it is that you are interested in accomplishing. Determine what type of business or clients will help you get there.

 WRITE IT

Q. 76 Why have you identified the above as your sweet spot?

You must be fully aware of "why" that is your target. Know it cold! Always maintain a realistic "wish list" of prospects. Constantly remind your team members of who your target prospect is. Include industry, plan assets, size of employee base, average employee compensation, proximity to your office and/or home etc. Make sure everyone in your target market knows that this segment is your specialty. You should maintain a good understanding of your sweet spot in the event that market conditions change. You need to be in a position to quickly respond to outside forces if the need arises.

Q. 77 Have you identified which type of business you are best suited to serve?

You should further clarify the type of client you are interested in attracting by asking yourself what type of companies you and your team could serve better than anyone else in the industry?

 WRITE IT

Q. 78 *What methods should I utilize to deliver my message to prospects and clients?*

Take your message to the street with any or all of the following:

- Direct efforts
- Networking
- Referrals
- Cold calling
- Cold walking
- Strategic partners
- Community professionals
- Direct mail
- Internet
- Centers of influence
- Workshops
- Seminars

Business Development

You have defined your target market within your marketing plan. Now that you know what you are looking for — the type of company, the range of employees, the asset base, etc., it's time to spring into action. In this section we will define how you will reach out to these prospects and describe methods for retaining them.

Q. 79 *How do I develop my acquisition activities?*

Review acquisition activities that you currently employ. Start with what you and your team members like to do, what has worked for you in the past and then add what you know that you can deliver well. Consider strategies suggested by others if you believe they may fill in any gaps you may have. Employ all acquisition strategies that you believe have a good probability of success. Consider all of the following: cold calling, cold walking, networking with community professionals, centers-of-influence, direct mail and workshops.

Q. 80 *How should I contact my prospects?*

Your contact management program could be designed to automate your direct mail, labels and even your e-mail. Your Marketing Plan outlines your strategy for contacting your prospects and your existing clients.

When prospecting, a combination approach may include: direct mail with e-mail and a follow-up telephone call or visit.

Utilizing multiple modes of contact, and delivering a consistent message will help you brand both you and your organization among the 401(k)/Company Retirement Plan decision-makers with whom you connect. You should know that your success will be built on your willingness to do what your competitors are unwilling to do. All modes of contact — direct mail, e-mail and follow-up calls — should convey the same theme to your prospect.

Q. 81 *How should I reach out to prospects?*

There are four major categories for continually keeping your message in front of the prospect. Those are:

- Electronic
- Print
- In-person
- Strategic partners (developed fully in Chapter 12)

We will look at each of these in greater depth and provide supporting ideas or examples.

Q. 82 *What do you suggest that we provide to our prospects and clients in electronic format?*

Web site — If it is possible for you to have a web site, do it. We have witnessed the power of the internet to provide greater opportunities to get your message out efficiently and communicate effectively to your prospects and clients. Just as the internet has grown, so have resources to help you to build your web presence. Conduct an internet search on "web site development" and you will see what we mean. If you do not have the skills and competencies to build your own site, absolutely contract with an accomplished designer who can build a web site that is best for you. Some topics to discuss with your web site designer include:

- Short site (home page)
- Long site (five or more pages)
- Do you want your site to be a "destination" for your prospects and clients? A destination site is one that your prospects and clients look forward to visiting again and again.
- What information do you want to make available to your prospects and clients from your site? Do you want to create a newsletter, or perhaps a "blog?"
- Link or not…that is the question. The use of links is a dynamic relationship and you should always obtain permission to link with other web sites. Some links you might want to consider include:
    - PLANSPONSOR magazine: www.plansponsor.com
    - The Department of Labor Employee Benefit Security Administration: www.dol.gov/ebsa
    - The Profit Sharing/401(k) Counsel of America: www.psca.org
    - The American Society of Pension Professionals and Actuaries: www.asppa.org
- Do you want your picture or the picture of your team on the site? What other artwork will be part of the page design?
- Who will host your web site?

E-mail "blasts" — The use of HTML within an e-mail "blast" is very effective. Your database of e-mail addresses needs to be current and robust. When used in conjunction with direct mail, e-mail blasts can build a lasting branding benefit. E-mail can be tracked and should provide measurable statistics for monitoring the effectiveness and success of each campaign.

Q. 83 *What do you suggest that we provide to our prospects and clients in print format?*

Brochure — In the marketing world a brochure is called a collateral piece, something that can stand on its own and communicate your message. A brochure is used to stimulate interest in you, your team and your services. In advertising you need to capture the reader's attention, create interest, generate desire, and compel the reader to take action.

The brochure for your business explains who you (or your team) are and the services that you provide. It can contain testimonials and other endorsements. It should reinforce your "brand," whether this is with a graphic, slogan or overall look. And your brochure must provide information on how the reader can learn more about you and your team as well as how to contact you.

Small brochures usually consist of one piece of paper folded into panels; they fit into a typical business-size envelope and are good for introductory overviews of your business. Larger brochures can consist of many pages stapled together; they provide room for more information and can make more of an impression, whether they are mailed or used as a "leave-behind" after a presentation.

If you hire a professional to develop your brochure, have a good idea of the minimum content you want included in the brochure. You will also want to have a process for evaluating the development firm and their work so that you can ensure that you are getting your money's worth. If you choose to go it alone and produce your own brochure, knowing what content you want is even more important.

Here are some design questions to consider:

- What is the purpose of the brochure?
- Who is your target audience?
- What is your message?
- Does your message include a reference to your Mission and Values (as outlined in Chapter 3)?
- Do you want to use graphics, testimonials, or examples of success?
- Does your brochure design capture the reader's attention immediately?
- Does the brochure cause the reader to be curious?
- Does it sufficiently stimulate the reader to seek additional information?

Production issues:
- Prepare rough copy and layout.
- Decide on one, two or four colors. Printing costs will depend on the number of colors used.

Contact a printer, preferably one that serves the professional services market. You want a printer that will provide guidance. If you do not have a good printer, ask a colleague, client or Chamber of Commerce for the names of printers that regularly work with professionals like you.

Position Piece — This is a one-pager, which should be easily drafted as the result of the development of your Vision-Mission-Values. (The Vision that you publish outside of your team may be a subset of the Vision that you developed with the group. You may choose to remove quantifiable language from your published version of the Vision.) The position piece document describes what you and your team deliver to the client and where you intend to take them. It should be an accurate representation of how you are going to satisfy the plan sponsor's 401(k)/Company Retirement Plan requirements. This one pager can be used in marketing and sales presentations to help you to communicate your great value and assist the decision-maker in answering the question, "Why should we choose you to serve us and our employees?" Here is sample text for a position piece. This is a good document for differentiating yourself and your team from your competitors:

> **Example:** *The Retirement Plan Group at ABC provides honest and forthright counsel in developing and delivering comprehensive solutions to (name of city/territory) based employers and their employees, assisting each to achieve their respective goals through their corporate retirement plan.*
>
> *We will assist our plan sponsor clients by enhancing the probability of their company's profitability through their company retirement plan. We will achieve this goal by assisting our plan sponsor clients to efficiently and effectively manage their fiduciary responsibility with respect to ERISA, and to make participants more aware of the benefit they are receiving from their employer.*
>
> *We will assist our plan participant clients to confidently accumulate and manage their retirement wealth. We will achieve this goal by helping plan participants to understand how their company retirement plan works to achieve their retirement savings goal. We will teach them how to effectively allocate their assets for retirement.*

Direct Mail "Drip" Campaign — All mailings should be followed up with a call to the addressee unless otherwise understood.

- Letters
- Articles of interest
- Workshop invitation
- Promotion of National 401(k) Day, sponsored by the Profit Sharing/401(k) Council of America, www.psca.org

Other types of print marketing can include:

- "Thank you" and holiday cards
- Newspaper advertising — "tombstone ad" after a "win"
- Invitations for sponsoring CPA events

Q. 84 *What do you suggest we provide to our prospects and clients in person?*

Speaking Engagements — Public speaking provides several benefits to your business. You can deliver your opinion on important 401(k)/Company Retirement Plan issues and present yourself as an "expert." Local civic organizations such as Rotary, Chamber of Commerce, Junior Chamber of Commerce, and industry related groups such as Human Resource Professionals, Treasurer and CFO groups are always seeking quality outside speakers. Develop a 20 minute presentation (with electronic presentation slides) which effectively delivers your message. Make sure to provide your bio to the individual who introduces you. Your bio is your first chance to make a good impression on your audience. How you are introduced — the information initially shared with the audience about you — sets the stage in their mind.

Sample presentations that you may want to have prepared include:

Presentations: General Public
- Managing Your 401(k) Account
- Will you Outlive Your Retirement Funds?
- Women and Investing

Presentations: Employees
* 401(k) Day
* Equity Investing
* Asset Allocation
* Market Volatility
* The Benefits of Participation

Specialized workshops for plan sponsors
* Brown-Bag Lunch Series of 401(k)
* Workshops for the General Public
* Referral lunches with clients
* Working lunches with clients and guest speaker; ERISA Attorney

Q. 85 *What marketing initiatives can I automate so that my database management system does the heavy lifting of marketing projects?*

There are major moments in the life of a 401(k)/Company Retirement Plan throughout the year. Besides communicating your service and current event themes in your direct mail letters, you may want to also consider working these "Major Moment" themes:

Plan audit: 1st quarter — A "fiduciary fear" approach that can also help you to promote your workshop entitled, "How to Survive a DoL Audit."

5500 preparation: 2nd quarter — Deadlines to submit 5500 forms are seven months following the end of the plan year, which is July 15th for calendar year end plans.

401(k) Day: 3rd quarter — Sponsored by the Profit Sharing/ 401(k) Council of America (www.psca.org), 401(k) Day is "...an annual celebration spotlighting the importance of employer-sponsored profit sharing and 401(k) plans." 401(k) Day officially falls on the day after Labor Day. You may choose another date that is more convenient for your work force. (Check out the Profit Sharing/401(k) Council web site and do what you can to promote 401(k) Day among your prospects as well as clients.)

Plan testing: 4th quarter — Offer to deliver employee education to "pump-up" the average deferral percentage of the non-highly compensated employees, reducing the chance of the plan failing discrimination testing and the highly compensated employees not being able to defer the amount they would prefer to contribute to their account.

Holiday / Thank You cards: 4th quarter

Q. 86 *There are many firms that offer to supply me with leads — is this a productive use of my time and resources?*

We offer... The "Good, the Bad, and the Reality" of purchased data and leads.

There are a variety of sources for obtaining data/leads. Each has different pricing with noticeably different value to the Financial Advisor.

Some who have been in the industry for over a couple of years include:

- www.401kexchange.com
- www.larkspurdata.com
- http://www.jda@freeerisa.com/

If you are considering the use of such an outside service we would advise you to fully understand your need before you purchase. There is a dramatic difference in the deliverables of firms in this business today. Deliverables range from a hard-copy list to pre-qualified leads (where the plan sponsor intends to conduct due diligence and move their plan to a new service provider within a set number of months).

The "Good"
- Efficient use of your time.
- Instantaneously you have at your disposal a universe of prospects.
- Prices vary — you should be able to find something within your budget.
- One of the organizations that you are (or your firm is) affiliated with may have access to such services at incremental cost.

The "Bad"

- No "monopoly": Many of your competitors will be working from a similar list (unless you are purchasing "leads"). Leads are usually sold to only one Financial Advisor — for obvious reasons.
- Most databases are derived from the same source — the 5500s supplied to the IRS by the plan sponsor.
- Purchased leads are expensive. If you close the business, however, there is no better value.
- Data can be six to 18 months old. Vendors are continually attempting to improve this, but part of the data collection process is out of their hands.
- Subject to the integrity of the data collection point and the data entry function.

The "Reality"

- There is no "silver-bullet" or "magic-wand"! With any purchased service, the Financial Advisor still needs to work hard at developing a plan and executing on that plan.
- No one can qualify a lead as well as you — and you build a relationship in the process!

Presentation Management

Q. 87 What are the presentations in your inventory?

At a bare minimum, you should always maintain a few presentations (with associated presentation media support.) These include:

- Discovery meeting
- Sales presentations
- Ongoing service

Q. 88 What do your presentations look like?

If you do not know, then shame on you! You must know!

Q. 89 Would you purchase a 401(k)/Company Retirement Plan from someone who demonstrates your presentation skills?

With the variety of technology available for creating audio-visual presentations, you must use it! It is imperative that you have an understanding of how you appear when presenting your services.

Q. 90 How accurately have you heard your presentations and how finely tuned are they?

When reviewing yourself on camera, look at it in three ways:

- How engaging am I?
- How convincing and credible is my story?
- What can I omit from my presentation?

Q. 91 How do you organize your sales presentation?

Prepare for the sales presentation by categorizing the information you discovered through the prospecting and profiling stages of interaction with your prospect. Begin by asking these questions:

- What are the priority points to discuss during the sales presentation?
- Who will participate in the sales presentation?
- Which employer representatives will be present?
- What are the audio/visual requirements?
- What is the sales presentation outline?

Once you have been notified by the prospect that you will be presenting, immediately inform your team members and any program provider reps that will be participating so that they can save the date on their schedule.

Your sales presentation outline may contain the following salient points:

- Opening
  - Thank the plan sponsor and trustees for the opportunity to present
  - Overview of timeline
  - List priority discussion points
  - Ask for confirmation of discussion points
- Presentation
  - Discussion points delivered by appropriate team members/program provider reps
- Closing
  - Leader summation
  - Next (or follow-up) steps
  - Why choose us
  - Thank attendees for their time

BEFORE the sales presentation, do the following:

- Practice your delivery. (REMEMBER, everything you do in front of the client *is* a presentation!)
- Verify what the plan sponsor wants to hear/see from you.
- If a search consultant is involved make sure to satisfy the consultant requirements.
- Practice the presentation with the other presenters from your firm (having a finely tuned presentation increases your odds of winning the business).

PRESENTATION DAY

- A/V check: Before you leave the office, try the audio and visual tools that you will use. Also, remember to protect your audio/ visual tools from extreme temperatures that could disrupt their operation.

- Time Check: For example, "We have prepared our presentation to last one hour as we were instructed. It is currently 2:10 p.m. We will go until 3:10 p.m."

    Do not allow time to be taken from your presentation if prior presenters exceeded their own allotted time. Decision makers should be aware that you are running a business and you want them to respect the time and effort that you and all other participants have put into the presentation.

Professional Development

We feel strongly that professional development is an absolute necessity for the 401(k)/Company Retirement Plan professional. Continuing education is required to retain your licenses. Enhancing your industry knowledge is important and new professional designations are introduced each and every year. These new and existing designations provide more choice than ever for Financial Advisors.

Keeping your edge by being a member of and participating in industry organizations is also advisable. To which organizations do you belong?

Professional Development is such an important aspect of your business that we have devoted Chapter 11 to the subject.

— C. Service —

Product Champion

Q. 92 *How can I stay abreast of changes to the 401(k)/Company Retirement Plan marketplace?*

What resources do you use to stay current with the employer-sponsored savings plan?

There are "direct" and "pass through" resources. Where are you getting your marketplace intelligence?

Please list any organizations that you belong to, local and national.

 WRITE IT

Client Retention Activities

Client retention activities are the heart of an organization. An organization needs to define service, document the service to be delivered, communicate to the client what service can be expected and then deliver the promised service.

Q. 93 How do you develop your retention activities?

Usually it is the lack of service or failure to meet an expectation that causes a client to search for a new program provider. Evaluate the quality of your client service and make improvements as necessary.

Ask your clients what they want you to do. Employers have good ideas, and they know what works for their employees. They may tell you that group meetings work best for certain employees and one-on-one meetings work better for others. They may allow you to submit articles for the company newsletter. They may fund a "Pizza Night" event so that employees can bring their spouse to hear you deliver a retirement savings message.

Having well-defined service strategies and delivery for employers (plan sponsors) and employees (plan participants) will mean the difference between satisfied long-term clients and clients who switch to another Financial Advisor. This service commitment is one area where your team can have the greatest impact on retaining the relationship. Define your strategies in your Business Plan so that you can both effectively communicate them and efficiently execute them.

The market will dictate a portion of your service deliverables and the corresponding quality. If you cannot match the level of service that your competitors are providing you need to introspectively question whether or not you should be in this line of business. Service expectations will also be dictated by your clients. Here again if you cannot meet the client's minimum expectations then you should ask yourself if the 401(k)/Company Retirement Plan business is one where you can compete?

If you are in a position to meet client expectations and match the service level of your competition, you have an excellent start on your retention activities. Retention activities should include your standard processes for servicing accounts and then some additional service.

These are areas where you *must* deliver — mediocre service is marginally better than no service at all. (Service Agreements are fully explained in Appendix A.)

Never underestimate the voice of the customer when attempting to service the customer. It is not your client's responsibility to remain your clients…it is your responsibility to keep them as clients!

Service Agreement

Q. 94 Who makes the decision to hire you and why?

Primary decision-making authority still remains with named trustees at the employer (yet more and more employers assemble committees with members from management and rank-and-file employees for decision making input.) Committee members are assuming a fiduciary function in assisting with the decision making process, so communicating your value during the acquisition phase to both employer and employees is important. When chosen, having well defined service strategies for employees will help you to effectively execute and manage your service activities.

 WRITE IT

Q. 95 How do you keep your clients happy?

Financial Advisors maintain a book of happy clients by under-promising and over-delivering on client expectations. What are you doing to over-deliver? When answering this question, think of what your competition delivers and compare that to what you deliver.

 WRITE IT

— D. Compliance —

Compliance is an entirely internal process, with each firm having its own "proprietary" requirements. You should always be sure that your initiatives and methodologies are within the compliance guidelines of your firm. Compliance guidelines within your firm provide great insight to accepted practices. You may be pleased to know that we have NOT devoted a chapter to compliance!

5

Assembling Your Team

One of the most important questions that a producer faces is whether to build a team or to remain a single Financial Advisor. There are a number of factors that will influence this decision, including:

- Your Vision (will a team help you to achieve it?)
- Compensation (can you afford to add staff; will they add to the bottom line?)
- Time management (will you have the time to effectively lead a team?)
- Efficiency (will adding people necessarily lead to enhanced productivity?)
- Ego (can you accept not being the biggest producer of the team?)
- Leadership (do you have the skills and temperament to lead?)

This list is not exhaustive, since each decision to expand or not is unique. However, the producer attempting to build a team should, at a minimum, consider these issues.

If, after careful consideration, you are certain in your conviction to remain a sole producer, then we suggest that you save your time and proceed to the next chapter. For those Financial Advisors who do intend to build a team, this chapter will be of great value to you.

There are multiple functions associated with managing your business. These include finance, sales, service, regulatory, compliance, and information technology. But, none of these will have the same "compounding" effect on your business as will the strong execution of a successful human capital acquisition and retention strategy — most frequently referred to as human resources. As a function of your business, human resources may seem mundane and time consuming. It is frequently assumed by the inexperienced to have a very low return on the time invested. We disagree with this viewpoint. Human resources should be seen as a strategic advantage for your business. The compounding effect of efficiencies generated by assembling a productive team may be the difference between success and failure. Hiring decisions are the first step in this process.

The well-worn investment disclaimer, "past performance is no guarantee of future results," also applies to potential employees. Even your best efforts to hire the right person may yield an employee who simply does not meet your requirements. There is some degree of luck involved. Nevertheless, you want to be sure that the process you use to vet the candidate is a sound one. This chapter includes a list that can serve as a template for your hiring process and we feel it is a good point of departure when interviewing candidates. Complement this list with any internal or corporate-office resources available and you can be confident that you have done everything possible to secure the very best team members.

Another very important aspect of the hiring process is your "gut-reaction." There is nothing that we can share with you here that will sharpen your ability to develop your instincts. We believe that the overwhelming majority of Financial Advisors are skilled in reading people and their true character. When you are engaged in the hiring process, do not ignore your gut-reaction to the person you are interviewing. If everything appears good on paper and the candidate interviews well, but you have a strong, uncomfortable feeling about them — keep looking (either spend more time with that candidate or begin looking at other candidates.) If you hire someone while ignoring a strong negative feeling about them you will, more often than not, be disappointed in some way. We are not referring to minor personality quirks, but major misgivings about the appropriateness of the candidate in question. Those of you who have hired staff in the past will know exactly what we are referring to. Those of you who are building a team and hiring for the first time will need to learn the value of your own gut-reaction over time.

Finally, be honest with yourself when evaluating your ability to recognize and attract the high quality talent that will make your team great, instead of just average. If you feel that you are not entirely up to the task, don't hesitate to seek professional advice.

Q. 96 *Should I hire support staff, Financial Advisors, or both?*

Your Strategic Plan and Business Plan (see Chapters Three and Four) will provide the answer to this question. What do you want to accomplish and what kind of employee(s) would help you to achieve your goals?

Q. 97 *What do I need to keep in mind when interviewing candidate team members?*

Will they be a contributor to the progress of the team or a drain on team resources? Will their knowledge and skills complement other team members? Can they adapt to the workload and succeed in a team environment?

Q. 98 *What questions should a team leader ask candidate team members?*

Make sure that you understand the corporate interviewing procedures and that you follow the appropriate organizational interviewing guidelines. If your firm has standard questions to ask, use them as well. State the specific job title for which the candidate is interviewing. Be prepared to provide an accurate job description to candidates so that they know what responsibilities you expect them to assume. The more accurate you are in articulating the expectations of the position and its corresponding responsibilities the more likely you are to secure the ideal new member for your team. If you speak only in generalizations, you may be continually hiring and rehiring for the same position.

Prior to your face-to-face interview session obtain a copy of the candidate's most recent resume. Take the time to review it *before* you sit across the desk from them. A good resume should provide you with sufficient material for discussion regarding the candidate's past experience and future aspirations.

The following are sample questions that we feel will provide every interviewer with valuable information:

Opening
- Please describe your general understanding of our business.
- Please describe your impression of how we service clients.
- Why are you interested in joining our team?
- What qualities are you looking for in our team and our firm?
- Please tell me about your formal education.

Work History
- Please tell me about your work history. (Begin with your oldest position to today.)
- Describe one or two of your major work related accomplishments.
- Why are you looking to leave your current position?
- What do you enjoy doing the most at your current job?
- What do you enjoy doing the least at your current job?

Job Performance
- What are the strengths that you will be bringing to this team?
- Describe the qualities of former supervisors with whom you have worked?
- Tell me about achievements for which you were recognized.
- What did you like most about your former supervisors?
- What did you like least about your former supervisors?
- What is the most important thing that you want from your job?
- What would your co-workers tell me about you?
- How do you stay abreast of changes in your job, industry?

Career Goals
- What are your career goals?
- What type of position do you see yourself holding three years from now?
- Do you have a three-year plan or goal?
- What do you need to assist you in achieving your three-year plan?
- Do you have a five-year plan or goal?

- If so, please describe your five-year goal or plan.
- What accomplishments (either work- or education-related) will help you to achieve your goal?
- How does this job fit into your long-term goal?
- What do you enjoy most about your profession?

Self-Assessment
- Tell me of a professional challenge which you addressed and overcame?
- What qualities would others mention when describing you?
- Describe what you feel has been your greatest professional achievement to date.
- What outcome of your work gives you the greatest feeling of satisfaction?

Decision Making
- What is your process for making a sound decision?
- What was the most difficult professional decision you made during last 12 months?
- Can you tell me of a situation either personal or professional when you had to make a dramatic change and how you addressed that situation?

Outside Interests
- What civic activities do you participate in?
- What fills your time when you are not working?

Motivation
- What motivates you?
- Describe for me one or two experiences on the job that provided you with a satisfying feeling. These would be experiences where you feel like you made a difference.

Work Standards
- When you observe peers who you believe are underachieving, what measures do you use in assessing their underperformance?
- Can you give me an example of how you organized others to accomplish a task?
- Describe someone you admire because of his or her work ethic.

Presentation Skills
- Do you enjoy presenting to a group?
- How do you prepare for presentations?
- Would you rather write a report or personally deliver material as a presentation?

Wrap-up
- Why should you become a part of our team?
- What questions do you have for me?

Q. 99 *What are the components of a job description?*

Job descriptions can contain the following information:

- Title of position
- Summarization of the position's role (maximum of two sentences)
- Definition of major responsibilities
- Listing of regular duties
- Listing of "extraordinary" duties

Keep in mind what the "career path" might be for this individual. Talk with the employee about what you see them accomplishing in one, three and five years. Give the employee your vision of their career path and the incremental steps to arrive at that vision.

Q. 100 *How do I determine which team member should be responsible for achieving specific tasks?*

There are administrative tasks and there are those tasks that only you can execute. If it is you and you alone, then you will be performing every task. If you are the leader of a team, then delegation and resource allocation become imperative. Do you share an administrative assistant? The bigger question is, "Are you willing and able to delegate tasks that you know that you should not be doing, and are you accepting those tasks that you know you should?"

You need to define the role and responsibilities of every member of your team. After doing so, delegate the appropriate tasks to the appropriate individual – based on their role and responsibilities.

The final step in making this happen is accountability. If you do not hold team members accountable, then you have only wasted your time in establishing expectations, and communicating those expectations. Remember, "there is no responsibility without accountability."

Q. 101 *How do I create a protocol to assess my team members?*

Assessment of team members is grounded within the job description for each position. This should include clearly defined roles and responsibilities. With that as a starting point, know whether you must follow an established corporate assessment method (performance cards, forms, checklist). If not, research different methods. Determine how often (quarterly, semi-annually, annually) you should review performance and what benchmarks you will use. Clearly communicate the performance assessment method to each team member so there is no question about how you will be evaluating them.

6
Your
Competition

Choosing where to compete is one of the most important strategic decisions you will make when entering the 401(k)/Company Retirement Plan market. There are a variety of factors that can influence your decision. Where you choose to compete will determine who your target market is as well as who your competitors will be. Some Financial Advisors choose markets based upon their own personal level of expertise and knowledge. Others select a market segment based on the firms that they would like to compete against; and yet others take guidance from their firms as to which market segments to pursue.

One strategy that will help you when competition is at hand (which is nearly always) is to clearly define the market you intend to serve. You can then select those program providers who support the market you are pursuing. Many program providers described their "sweet spot" as every plan between $1 million and $500 million. Anyone who has been in the business any length of time is fully aware that such a statement is folly. In theory it may be an enviable achievement, however it borders on the absurd. No one can specialize in an arena so broad.

Remember that competition is healthy. Competition makes every one of us better at what we do. Without competition, plan sponsors and plan participants would be left in the dark ages on plan services, features and innovation.

Q. 102 *Where (in what asset base) should I decide to compete?*

There are major differences in the sale and servicing of various segments of the 401(k)/Company Retirement Plan industry. Clear distinctions of market descriptions and variations occur among the following segments:

- Start-up – $750,000
- $750,000 – $5 million
- $5 million – $50 million
- $50 million – $500 million
- Over $500 million

An individual or a firm entering the 401(k)/Company Retirement Plan market must decide in which of these market segments to compete. The skill sets required of an individual who services the $1 million plans will be substantially different than the skill sets required of an individual who has elected to service the $350 million plan market. (See Chapter 8 for more detail on the different market segments.)

If you are in the process of determining where to compete, or considering a move to compete in a larger market, we suggest that you approach peers, wholesalers of program providers who serve that market segment as well as individuals and firms you will be competing against. It benefits you to have many lengthy conversations with these professionals to understand their experience and guidance. These conversations can put you in the position to best determine if you will be able to match the selling skills and technical expertise exhibited by your future competitors. You will also learn if the product or services that you intend to offer can stand up to the competition.

Conducting the proper research at the front end of your target market search can save you from years of banging your head against the wall in a market where neither you nor your product belong.

Q. 103 **Which companies or Financial Advisors in your territory do you compete against on a regular basis?**

As you have probably noticed, you frequently compete against the same Financial Advisors, firms and program providers for your "target" plans. Successful 401(k)/Company Retirement Plan Financial Advisors have an excellent knowledge and understanding of the individuals and the products against which they compete. If you do not have a thorough understanding of what the competition offers in your marketplace, make it a priority to acquire that knowledge. (If this task appears too broad then narrow it down to the top three 401(k)/ Company Retirement Plan competitors in your industry market segment [i.e. $5 million – $50 million]. For the remainder of the questions in this chapter, always consider [at a minimum] your top three competitors.)

 WRITE IT

Q. 104 What qualities do these organizations or individuals possess that make them so competitive?

Look hard at your competition. Are they successful in a single market or are they successful across a single product line? Is their success due to national advertising, regional presence, the quality of individuals who are working for the firm or is there some other reason they are so successful?

 WRITE IT

Q. 105 What traits are consistently exhibited by strong competitors in your area?

Observe the traits that are noticeably demonstrated and repeated by your strong competitors. If you have no way of directly observing these traits or behaviors you will need to obtain that information in some other manner. But do keep in mind, if you intend to rise to that level, you must obtain high-quality competitive intelligence.

 WRITE IT

Q. 106 *How do I acquire high quality competitive intelligence?*

Hopefully your values prohibit you from engaging in any nefarious practices to gain intelligence. The best methodology we know of for gaining intelligence is interviewing the clients of your stiffest competition. (Remember, good competitors will make you better!) Interviewing your competitor's clients can provide the knowledge that you seek. Ask your prospects that are currently using a top competitors program the following:

- Why they chose the program
- Why they selected their Financial Advisor
- What they would change

Q. 107 *Can I successfully differentiate myself in the area of investments when so many plan sponsors view the plan investments as a commodity?*

In most cases, Financial Advisors have access to the same investment lineup. If you choose to compete on investments alone you will have a very difficult time differentiating your product from that offered by your competition. You may find yourself constantly defending what you offer as opposed to leading with what you can do for the plan sponsor and the plan participants. Be proactive versus reactive! Do not attempt to differentiate yourself by competing solely the on the basis of your investment products. Outstanding service is what will set you apart.

Q. 108 **Does any current news or article from a national, regional or local publication impact your competitor's relationship with their plan sponsor?**

Anytime a competitor receives press coverage it definitely has the potential to impact the relationship they have with their plan sponsor clients. Look objectively at the topics, the tone and the substance of what the press is focusing on. You will undoubtedly be asked in the marketplace for your opinion of what has appeared in the press. Be able to demonstrate that you have an awareness of the situation, but be careful not to disparage your competitors. You are better off separating yourself from the competition by rising above them rather than by attempting to push them down. (Keep in mind that someday you or your firm may be in the press as well!)

Q. 109 What resources does the competition use to stay current with the 401(k) market?

The simplest way to obtain this information is to ask your competition directly. In the chapter on Professional Development (Chapter 11), we list some of the publications and resources that we feel you should subscribe to and utilize. However, because new publications and services are frequently introduced to the market, never underestimate the value of the direct question to a friendly competitor, "What does your team use to stay current on today's 401(k)/Company Retirement Plan issues?"

 WRITE IT

Q. 110 Describe in three sentences or less how your current program differs from each of your top three competitors.

Can you do it? Can you do it without berating the competition? If not, refine your statements so that they build you and your program up without slamming the competition. If you cannot accurately describe your product and service differences in three sentences or less, you must work to accomplish that. Hopefully you will be in a position quite frequently to compare yourself favorably to the competition.

 WRITE IT

Q. 111 How does this compare to how your competition describes their service to your prospects/clients?

If you do not know this, get to work! You must understand how your top three competitors are presenting themselves to your prospects/ clients. Even if the competition approaches your clients, remember, they are *your* clients. You should have a strong enough relationship with your clients to obtain such information.

Section II –
Product
Awareness

7

Basic Retirement Plan Knowledge

For the Financial Advisor who is starting a 401(k)/Company Retirement Plan business, the challenges are many. There is an endless supply of detail and minutia. Someone new to the business could spend 100 days straight studying and still have plenty to learn. One of the earliest challenges a Financial Advisor may face is gaining the confidence required to become conversant with CEOs, CFOs, and other decision makers around retirement plan issues.

An inexperienced Financial Advisor may be reluctant to enter this market due to the volume of material that must be learned. A hurdle for everyone entering this business is the question, "How much am I expected to know concerning design, administration, investments, recordkeeping and fiduciary issues?" There is a fine line between spending too much or too little time learning the detail. Eventually you will reach a point of "diminishing returns." We would not go so far as to say that your time is wasted, however, we would question the number of additional prospects you could bring in or your ability to deliver service at a higher level due to this detailed background.

When you are posed with a retirement plan question, you can respond truthfully, respond falsely or respond inaccurately (all the while believing that your answer *is* accurate). By responding truthfully, you build trust and confidence with the plan sponsor. Responding falsely (whether through ignorance or embarrassment) could come back to haunt you, either later with a client or much later in your career. Never be reluctant to use the response "I do not know, but I will research your question, find the correct answer and get back to you as quickly as possible." This builds trust and confidence with most plan sponsors — as long as you follow through. You enhance your reputation when you go the extra mile to provide an accurate and thorough response. The technical side of this business can change with every new system, law or investment offering. Depending on the market in which you are competing, you will be expected to know different levels of each. However, you must know your product thoroughly. You must always be in a position to share how your product can address any challenge that the plan sponsor faces.

Always remember these three things — and accept them as fact:

- No one knows everything.
- Unfortunately, this includes you!
- Plan sponsors appreciate honesty.

If you are new to this business and question whether or not you have all of the required knowledge to begin making calls, consider soliciting the help of someone in your office or a strategic partner. Have a mentor or strategic partner work with you on one or two plans, so that you can build your confidence to a level that positions you to close 401(k)/Company Retirement Plan business.

There are some basics that you should be aware of — those follow next. Just a word before we get into it. Don't sweat the details! Many of them are covered in greater depth later and some will not even be your responsibility. Get a handle on the bigger picture first.

Q. 112 *What are the major components of a retirement plan business?*

There are multiple descriptions for the major components of a 401(k)/Company Retirement Plan. You need a logical hierarchy when describing the major components. The following hierarchy can be used when describing 401(k)/Company Retirement Plans:

- Design
- Administration
- Investments
- Recordkeeping

• Employee Communications
• Trustee/Fiduciary

Every task, process or unit of work within a 401(k)/Company Retirement Plan can logically fall under one of the above major components.

Q. 113 *What does design include?*

With each and every tax qualified retirement plan a formal plan document exists. This document will outline the various provisions of the plan. Topics such as employee eligibility and employee entry dates into the plan (and a variety of additional nuances) are contained within the document. Also addressed in plan design are plan sponsor matching contributions, profit sharing contributions, safe harbor contributions and cross-tested allocations. If document design is a new concept to you then you should read through at least one existing plan document to make yourself familiar with the verbiage and structure.

Q. 114 *What does administration include?*

Administration encompasses the day-to-day management of the plan. All management of the plan should be according to both the plan document and the Employee Retirement Income Security Act of 1974 (ERISA). Administration may include compliance testing, telephone support with the plan sponsor, preparation of forms (1099 and 945), preparation of distribution checks, acceptance of payroll data, loan processing, late notice memorandum for delinquent loans, processing changes for deferral rates, processing of qualified domestic relations orders, maintaining beneficiary data, identification of newly eligible employees and the preparation of Form 5500.

Q. 115 *What does recordkeeping include?*

Recordkeeping includes all of the plan investment transactions (including participant directed investments) and the sub-accounting for plan participants as well as the rollup of that sub-account data to the master trust account. All participant account balances will be maintained at the recordkeeping level. Over 85 percent of 401(k) plans employ a daily recordkeeping system. In a daily environment the record keeper is able to accurately report end-of-day balances to each individual plan participant. The recordkeeping unit will also prepare written statements to be sent to plan participants either quarterly, semiannually or annually. (The advent of the Internet has rendered the participant statement obsolete for obtaining the most up-to-date account balance information.) The recordkeeping unit also manages telephone inquiries initiated by plan participants and maintenance of the Internet connection. Some recordkeeping units will make available, via the Internet or telephone request, a report reflecting a participant's personalized rate of return.

Q. 116 *What does employee communications include?*

The level of employee communication is dependent upon the type of plan (401[k], defined benefit, ESOP, etc.). However, employee communication is vitally important for every 401(k) plan. Any and every participant-directed 401(k) plan will require the highest level of employee communication. It is logical that if a participant will be directing the investment of their account balances, then the plan sponsor will want to insure that every plan participant has access to high quality information upon which to base their investment decisions. For participant-directed plans, quarterly or semi-annual education meetings are typically delivered by a Financial Advisor or member of a program provider support team.

Q. 117 *What is the function of a trustee?*

Trustee is probably the most misunderstood function of the 401(k) plan. The function of a trustee is to safeguard the assets. Loosely defined, safeguarding the assets means that the assets will be available to the participant for their intended use, at the appropriate time. Trustees have and will always maintain a fiduciary interest in the plan, plan assets and plan participants. A trustee is held to the highest standard of accountability. The majority of 401(k)/Company Retirement Plans are self-trusteeships, meaning that one or more employees (owner, CEO, Committee, etc.) at the sponsoring organization is the plan trustee. When an outside organization (program provider, bank, etc.) is appointed trustee, then that organization serves in the capacity of a corporate trustee.

Q. 118 *How much time should I spend learning design?*

As with all of the major categories associated with 401(k) plans, you can spend as much time as you want, delving deeper and deeper into the plan design. For those of you who desire to best serve the plan participants, we again recommend that you seek advice from a highly qualified ERISA counsel either inside or outside your firm. Spend time on the basics yourself. If you are serious about making the retirement plan business your specialty, we recommend a three- to five-day class offered by an industry organization or association. Doing so should give you sufficient background to be in a position to help plan sponsors with the obvious issues.

Q. 119 *How much time should I spend learning administration?*

The answer to this question will vary depending on the type of firm you represent and the extent to which you will be dealing with administrative tasks. In either case it would benefit you to spend a day sitting next to a knowledgeable individual who works exclusively in plan administration. By working side-by-side for a full day you can get exposure to the majority of issues that a true 401(k)/Company Retirement Plan administrator faces. One of the program providers that you intend to work with may be helpful to you in this effort. If you are responsible for growing the 401(k)/Company Retirement Plan business, your function will be different from that of an administrator. It is valuable to know what they do, but it is not necessary to know how they do it.

Q. 120 *How much time should I spend learning investments?*

Lots! We said earlier that you do not want to compete on investment products alone. That is still true. However, an extensive knowledge of the investment world and appropriate investments for 401(k)/Company Retirement Plans may be the point that differentiates you from the competition. We are not referring to specific investments. As we said, the investments offered in a plan are almost commodities. Where you will differentiate is in your knowledge of asset allocation, diversification, modern portfolio theory, etc. Prudent investment management concepts and your ability to accurately articulate your expertise can make a difference to the plan sponsor. Spend a major portion of your time becoming comfortable with investments and the investment function. Plan on seven to 20 hours per week.

Q. 121 *How much time should I spend learning recordkeeping?*

Initially you should spend three to five hours getting comfortable with the capabilities and reports available through your recordkeeping system. After that, one hour per quarter should be sufficient to stay current with regulatory requirements and your system enhancements. Do not get bogged down with recordkeeping. You want to speak knowledgeably on the subject, but you do not need to know every intricate detail of the system.

Q. 122 *How much time should I spend learning employee communication?*

A bunch! Employee communication can be the difference between a short relationship and a very long-term and profitable relationship. The plan sponsor has spent substantial time and corporate cash to install the 401(k)/Company Retirement Plan for the benefit of the employees. Your target audience for employee communication consists of every eligible plan participant. You must strive to keep every one them satisfied. In the meantime, you must keep the executive team at the plan sponsor excited about having you on their account. Depending upon the market you serve and the program providers that your firm supports, you may spend anywhere from 10 to 30 hours per week in front of plan participants.

Q. 123 *How much time should I spend learning the aspects of trusteeship?*

Some. Many individuals who are your competitors do not have a full understanding of the role of a trustee/fiduciary. This would be an excellent area in which to devote some additional time. With concentrated study you should be able to comprehend the relationship and responsibility of a trustee within 10 to 20 hours. The good news is the trustee concept is like a light switch; it's either on or off. It's completely different from investments or administration where things can change every day. You may consider classes to improve your fiduciary awareness if you wish to learn the business quickly.

Q. 124 *With so many components of 401(k)/Company Retirement Plans, how do I know where to concentrate my time?*

Determine which of the major components — design, administration, investments, recordkeeping, employee communications or trustee/fiduciary — need your attention the most. In which of these areas are you weakest and in which are you the strongest? Your Vision and your Mission should help you identify the areas most in need of improvement. Self-assessment is difficult enough, but accurate self-assessment is very difficult indeed. Consider asking someone from your firm to interview you on these topics to help you decide where to focus your efforts.

Q. 125 *What resources are available to help me become proficient in plan design?*

Visit the following web sites in order to improve your knowledge and awareness of plan design:

- www.psca.org (Profit Sharing/401(k) Council of America)
- www.ebri.org (Employee Benefit Research Institute)
- www.asppa.org (The American Society of Pension Professionals and Actuaries)
- www.dol.gov/ebsa (Department of Labor, Employee Benefit Security Administration)

Q. 126 *What resources are available to help me become comfortable with the investment function?*

To improve your knowledge and awareness of plan investments, visit the following web sites:

- www.morningstar.com
- http://www.styleanalysis.com
- www.ibbotson.com

- www.wsj.com
- http://online.barrons.com/public/main/

Also, identify, locate and meet at least two (more if possible) investment professionals in your geographic area whose professional opinion you respect. For you to gain maximum benefit, these individuals should be free thinkers who frequently disagree with you, challenge your assumptions and possess different points of view.

Q. 127 *What resources are available for becoming comfortable with employee communication?*

- www.newkirk.com
- http://www.investmenthorizons.com
- www.kmotion.com

Q. 128 *What resources are available for becoming comfortable with the administrative functions of a plan?*

- www.asppa.org
- http://www.mhco.com
- www.plansponser.com
- www.newkirk.com
- ERISAFACTS (publication)

Q. 129 *Where might I get lost in attempting to learn everything about 401(k)/Company Retirement Plans?*

It is best to first understand the topics associated with each of the major components (design, administration, investments, recordkeeping, employee communications, and trustee) before attempting to analyze any one specific product. Do not select the program provider before you attempt to understand the components of the specific program or you will most likely get lost in the detail.

When considering which program to deliver, it is best not to get bogged down in the minutia. Eventually it may be appropriate to learn that level of detail — but not until then.

8

Retirement Plan Basics, But a Little Deeper

Identifying which segment of the market you intend to serve will guide you in determining the appropriate depth of knowledge you must acquire, and to what extent you will need to comprehend the detail needed for acquiring and servicing 401(k)/Company Retirement Plans. It will also help you to understand at what depth the major components of a retirement plan must be understood. In the retirement plan community a widely accepted structure of products and services is design, administration, investments, recordkeeping, employee education, and trusteeship. (Another structure may work better for you.) If you participate in the jumbo market segment, you will need to have a clear understanding of all major sub-systems associated with each of the above-mentioned topics. If you participate in the middle market then you will not be required to have as much in-depth knowledge of these sub-systems. If you participate at the micro level of the market you will be expected to know less about specific product delivery. However you will still be expected to have a broad knowledge of the wide variety of 401(k)/Company Retirement Plan programs offered throughout the industry.

Q. 130 Which market segment are you currently serving?

For purposes of this question, assume there are five major market segments:

- Start-up – $750,000
- $750,000 – $5 million
- $5 million – $50 million
- $50 million – $500 million
- over $500 million

Start-up – $750,000 — In this market you, the Financial Advisor, will be expected to know which one of the many program providers, products and services will best fit the intermediate needs of the company. You also must be compensated fairly for the work that will be conducted on the plan. In most cases you will not get consumed by specific tasks or activities involved with the administration of the plan. At this level you will be very involved in investment selection as well as employee communication and ongoing education. In the past, the conversation between you and the plan sponsor was usually devoid of questions related to trustee issues. Recently there has been a heightened awareness around fiduciary issues at this level, due to the fact that owners of smaller companies are very interested in protecting all of their assets in a prudent manner.

$750,000 – $5 million — This market normally represents a plan in transition. Frequently this plan will have been established with the very first program provider that the company selected in their startup phase. If you are fortunate enough to find a plan this size that is still with their original vendor, you should be able to improve service to plan participants and lower overall fees and expenses for the plan sponsor. More service options are available to plan participants at this level as well. As the Financial Advisor, you will have access to multiple program providers. Product and service delivery knowledge are major assets that you bring to the plan sponsor. Fees and expenses can be difficult for the plan sponsor to understand and part of your function should be to help them comprehend all costs. You will still be intricately involved in the investments and employee communications. The time required for a small company to spend on the administration of a plan of this size will be a factor to the plan sponsor buyer. Smaller companies do not have internal resources sufficient to dedicate one individual full-time to 401(k)/Company Retirement Plan administration.

$5 million – $50 million — At this segment of the market the Financial Advisor needs to be more conversant and knowledgeable than at any other previously mentioned market segment. The Financial Advisor who serves this segment enters into in-depth conversations with plan sponsors along each of the major categories (design, administration, investments, recordkeeping, employee communications, and trustee.). With a 401(k)/Company Retirement Plan of this size you will most likely work with a group or a committee. "Groupthink" is a much different sales and selection process than selling to one individual. Generally you will need to satisfy anywhere from two to ten committee members throughout the decision process. In this size plan, every design decision will have a financial impact on the plan and possibly on the operating company. Some companies will have a full-time employee responsible for managing the 401(k)/Company Retirement Plan. Therefore, the questions coming from that individual will require more detailed answers about the administrative operations of the plan. Frequently plans of this size will include involvement of the human resources director, chief financial officer, and other treasury professionals with decision-making responsibilities. At this point the plan participants will have made it clear to their employer what is deficient on participant statements, the face-to-face education or investment advice. The sophistication level of trustee/fiduciary parties is not consistent throughout this segment of the market; this gives you the opportunity to add great value by demonstrating your vast knowledge of the subject.

$50 million – $500 million — Within this market segment the selling landscape changes dramatically. It is highly unlikely that you will be expected to possess specialist knowledge in each and every one of the major categories when dealing with plans of this size. In this segment you will be in a position to rely on specialists associated with service providers in their support roles. You will not be required to have the depth of knowledge on specific programs as you would for smaller plans. At this level you begin to operate more as the quarterback of the selling team, ensuring that everyone is working to accomplish the same goal. At this level you must be adept at assembling the correct lineup. Once the lineup is established, the group needs to perform impeccably when given their 90 minutes in front of the selection team or plan retirement committee. In this market segment you will most likely be presenting to between five and twelve committee members. Since you will be surrounded by specialists during the presentation, you yourself will field fewer questions. Once again, your role is to prepare everyone in your group for what they are about to encounter. When in front of the customer with your group, demonstrate your capabilities, interest and understanding of what is required to successfully deliver your products and services to the plan sponsor and their employees.

Over $500 million — Within the jumbo market the selling environment is completely different. A Financial Advisor/dedicated salesperson will be leading with a very specific single product solution. Although there is a tremendous amount of flexibility in what can be promised and delivered for acquiring a plan of this size, there will be no deviation from the platform that the program provider utilizes. Usually, the Financial Advisor/salesperson at this level is not required, nor will they have much need, to understand much of the detail in the delivery of the plan. These individuals are strong in design and communication. At this level, the ability to deliver services to every plan participant, with little to no variation, is what plan sponsors desire most. The trustee and fiduciary issues have a heightened importance at this level. The individual who serves this market will spend as much time learning their own internal systems as they do learning the industry.

As you can see, each of these category segments requires different skill sets and levels of service for the Financial Advisor. The categories provide an overview of how the competition will change and how you must adapt if you intend to move up- or down-market. It is safe to say that there may be some variations to what is described above, but as a broad generalization, this is what you can expect to encounter.

Q. 131   In what capacity will you be serving your clients?

You should have a clear understanding of your role in serving your clients. You could serve as a registered investment advisor, which means you will have a fiduciary responsibility to the plan participants and plan fiduciaries. You may serve as broker of record, which does not carry the same level of documented fiduciary responsibility. Serving as third-party administrator would relieve you of most of the investment responsibility. If acting as an insurance agent, different state-by-state regulation must be considered. Come to a clear understanding of what obligations you have in regard to your plan participants, plan fiduciaries and sponsor/client.

Q. 132   What part of the product will you be delivering versus overseeing?

The more clearly you can communicate your individual involvement and control over their plan (assets and process) the more you increase the likelihood that the client will buy from you. A big factor in having satisfied clients is in properly establishing their expectations. (The Service Agreement, discussed in Appendix A, will help you establish client expectations). Ultimately, you are responsible for the smooth operation of the plan at all levels. When a service breakdown occurs your client will look to you for a solution. You should assume ownership of any process or system failure in the product. (Different firms will have various limits on how much ownership you are permitted to assume. You must remain consistent with the direction and limits of your firm and *always* be in compliance.) If you will be negatively impacted by the service shortcomings, then you must be sure that the entire system functions as close to flawlessly as possible. Any 401(k)/Company Retirement Plan program provider can make a "one-off" mistake. If the same program provider makes the same mistake on multiple plans then either their process is flawed or their input is corrupt. In either event you can ill-afford to deliver another plan to that program provider until you are confident that the root cause of their mistake has been eliminated.

Q. 133 Do you have the knowledge and system controls to recognize when there is an operational malfunction that impacts your clients?

You must take the time to ensure that you possess the fundamental knowledge required to properly manage the client relationship. This includes understanding those areas that are critical to the plan's success or failure. At a minimum, you should comprehend the following: funding requirements, reporting requirements, compliance requirements and Department of Labor requirements. The client depends on you for absolutely everything. You will become known as the person who handles everything on the plan. Although you will not perform every task for the plan, you must have adequate systems and processes in place to recognize when the plan is failing to meet your client's needs or expectations. Once you are alerted to such failures, your immediate response should be twofold: 1) notify the program provider of the problem, and 2) take corrective action on behalf of your customer.

Q. 134 *In today's ever-changing competitive environment, which product should I choose to deliver to clients?*

There is no easy answer. Which product/program provider you select for your client will be determined by your knowledge of the alternatives, cross-referenced with the availability of that product to your firm and "seasoned" with your experience of both the vendor and client. (Unless you only have one product to offer — in which case you can move to the next question.)

The selection of a specific product for a client becomes an art. Some program providers are excellent for a specific client industry; others are better suited for a specific client size. If you are new at this business, you should spend a fair amount of time interacting with other 401(k)/Company Retirement Plan professionals to obtain their opinion on program providers. You may benefit by speaking with 401(k)/Company Retirement Plan professionals who are affiliated with your firm but do business outside of your geographic target market. Be aware, some program providers promote their product to the plan sponsor community as the best solution for everyone and every client demographic. Unfortunately, such a product does not exist. Also be aware that some competitor firms will place more emphasis on past experiences while your personal experiences may wind up being quite different.

You should know of at the least three excellent programs for the market you serve. It may benefit you to also be aware of two excellent systems for the next tier up from the segment in which you participate.

Q. 135 Which 401(k)/Company Retirement Plan program providers do you favor and what are their program qualities that you stress to prospects?

Give careful consideration to how a particular program provider matches your personal and professional strengths. We encourage you to conduct interviews with program providers.

You should inform the plan sponsor that you are in a strong position to conduct due diligence on 401(k) plan program providers.

You should represent competitive programs and compete on service.

Program providers want what you want, they just assess its value differently.

Program providers tend to be more pragmatic than Financial Advisors in assessing the attractiveness of a 401(k) plan. Whereas a particular plan may enable you to make a profit within the first year of its implementation, a program provider may require several years to reach profitability.

Economies of scale apply to the Financial Advisor as well as program providers, but each of you have different and dynamic formulas for achieving economies of scale. So not every program provider wants to or can deliver what you need to best serve the client.

Q. 136 *What do clients need to comprehend concerning the Statement of Investment Policy?*

The Statement of Investment Policy provides the comfort of employing a process around the investment function. As long as a plan sponsor utilizes a sound process for selecting, monitoring and evaluating plan investments there should be a limited number of investment related struggles. You should make yourself familiar with the SIP offered by your firm or by a program provider.

Q. 137 *What else should I know?*

We have listed some of the topics that will help in your sales efforts in the 401(k)/Company Retirement Plan market. These are not so much technical terms as much as they are talking points during your prospecting sessions and sales calls. They should help you establish where a plan sponsor may have problems with their 401(k)/Company Retirement Plan and demonstrate the difference between you and the competition. Those points include:

Participation Rates — You should be able to look at a plan's demographic data and determine if you are in a position to increase participation among the lower paid employee base.

Employee Education — Find out about the education effort that has taken place in the past and use it as a baseline. You will then determine if you are in a position to improve upon it.

History of the Plan — It is always useful to spend some time discussing what has occurred in the company retirement plan in prior years. This will provide perspective as you look to improve the overall 401(k)/Company Retirement Plan.

Goals for the Plan and Plan Participants — Knowing what goals have been established for the plan sponsor and plan participants provides valuable information as you attempt to learn the plan sponsor's expectations.

Participant Meetings — Gaining a clear understanding of what has been expected of the existing Financial Advisor is helpful in determining if you can satisfy this client in the long-term.

Quarterly or Annual Plan Review or Investment Meetings — This is an area where you need to take control of the program. Once again, understanding what was delivered in the past and using this as a baseline should position you to establish expectations and exceed them in the future.

9

What the Client Wants (versus What the Client Needs)

There are always two client groups with any 401(k)/Company Retirement Plan, the plan sponsor and the plan participants. Each of these unique client groups has specific interests in the plan. Some of the interests of each group are shared and some are in direct conflict. For example, an employer may want to contribute the minimum amount required, which would permit the highly compensated employees to maximize their own deferrals, while the rank and file (non-highly compensated employees) prefer the maximum contribution permissible.

The traditional 401(k) plan features participant direction of investments. The investment management function of traditional defined benefit plans is controlled at the trustee level. In the traditional defined benefit plan, communication of plan benefits to plan participants is a very important annual event for the plan sponsor. Within the 401(k) structure, participant education with regard to investments is an ongoing operation. In many plans, the participant education process occurs haphazardly, if at all. Such a scenario can create a situation in which the plan participants are unhappy with their results while the owner of the company or the executive team feels that everything is fine. You must always keep foremost in your mind that you are the specialist, working first for the plan participants and then the plan sponsor. You will be everyone's go-to person for any questions that arise on the plan or the investments.

Your clients will have an idea of what they would like to obtain from the 401(k)/Company Retirement Plan. One of your major challenges in this business is to marry your client's desires with their real needs. Some plan sponsors have unrealistic expectations, but your job is still to provide a plan that meets their needs.

Within a 401(k)/Company Retirement plan you have the opportunity to develop satisfied clients while at the same time developing cross-selling opportunities. What could be better? You are helping plan sponsors achieve corporate objectives, assisting those plan sponsors' employees in realizing their retirement funding dreams — all while receiving compensation. Yours is an honorable profession. Seize this opportunity; become the best at knowing what your clients (both groups) need, and use that information to achieve your goals. Your clients must have "ownership" in the relationship. This can be demonstrated by their sharing their goals and abilities with you. Also effectively communicating via ongoing feedback will help you fine-tune your service for the client and participant's benefit.

In this chapter we will address only the plan sponsor as client. We will address the plan participants as client in Chapter 15.

— Client Wants —

Q. 138 *How do I determine what the client wants?*

Ask your plan sponsor/client what they would like the plan to accomplish. The question here is twofold; you are not only interested in what the plan sponsor would like the plan to accomplish for the company, but also what the plan sponsor would like the plan to accomplish on behalf of the plan participants. (Never lose sight of the fact that you have those two client segments within a 401(k)/Company Retirement plan.) Some plan sponsors will be fully aware of and ready to express their needs. With others you might have to work a little harder to obtain the answers.

Q. 139 *How do I determine plan sponsor/client's real desires?*

You probe deeper and go beyond the superficial response that a plan sponsor may give you when you ask the question, "What do you want this plan to accomplish for you?" Look for answers that are two or three levels deep from the first response. For example:

>**You:** *What do you want this plan to accomplish for your company?*
>**Plan sponsor:** *We want to offer an employee benefit to our team members.*
>**You:** *Why do you want to offer a 401(k) plan as an employee benefit?*
>**Plan sponsor:** *Everybody else is doing it.*
>**You:** *Do you see your offering the 401(k) plan as a competitive advantage?*
>**Plan sponsor:** *We see it as survival. Without such a plan we have no ability to acquire the highly skilled people that we need.*

This type of questioning, probing and re-questioning will build a better understanding of the plan sponsor/client's desires.

Q. 140 *What is the number one client request?*

1) "I want happy, appreciative and productive employees."

Q. 141 *What are numbers two, three and four?*

2) "I have no time or resources available to spend on administration."
3) "I want zero responsibility for investments."
4) "I do not want fees being charged back to the company."

Q. 142 *What is the fifth client request?*

5) "I want to assume zero fiduciary responsibility."

These responses, given by actual plan sponsors, reveal their true feelings. You will notice that some of the responses are masks for deeper underlying issues. Let's take them in order.

1) "I want happy, appreciative and productive employees."
This is difficult to disagree with and we believe this to be a reasonable request to the extent that the 401(k)/Company Retirement Plan can help accomplish that goal.

2) "I have no time or resources available to spend on administration."
This is probably a true and accurate statement, however what most plan sponsors mean when making such a statement is, "I do not want to continually correct your mistakes. I do not want to involve our own people or resources in performing tasks which are repetitive and able to be automated."

3) "I want zero responsibility for investments."
One of the perceived benefits of offering participant directed investments to employees was that of removing the plan sponsor from the investment decisions. Many plan sponsors state that they do not want to be responsible for investments, but they will not take the proper steps to protect the plan participants, which would ultimately protect themselves. In most cases there is a false sense of security that by simply offering participant directed accounts, the plan sponsor is shielded from, and absolved of, any investment responsibility.

4) "I do not want fees being charged back to the company."
Plan sponsors who turn a blind eye toward the fees and expenses associated with "other people's money" are creating a liability for plan fiduciaries. What the plan sponsor wants is understandable, but unrealistic. It is possible to manage expenses in such a way that sponsorship of the plan is still a competitive advantage for the company.

5) "I want to assume zero fiduciary responsibility."
This statement is true — plan sponsors have little interest in participating in the fiduciary arena. Okay. For those of you who are familiar with fiduciary responsibility, you undoubtedly recognize the absurdity associated with "burying your head in the sand" from a fiduciary perspective. This is an incredibly dangerous attitude, and surprisingly, it is shared by tens of thousands of plan fiduciaries.

— Client Needs —

The "needs" we highlight within this chapter are based upon our experience and exposure to best practices. These "needs" are not based upon legal requirements. We suggest that you recommend to your clients that they always have ERISA counsel review their plan and documentation supporting their plan.

Within the remainder of this Chapter we use language such as "you must." Again, this is not based upon legal requirements, but rather on what we have witnessed to be necessary to have a successful 401(k)/ Company Retirement Plan business.

Q. 143 *How do I determine what the plan sponsor/client needs?*

You should already be aware of 95% of a plan sponsor's needs before you begin to serve them. Plan sponsors have specific needs that fall under the categories of:

- Regulatory
- Operational
- Communications
- Investments
- Fiduciary

Your job is to understand the impact of each of these categories upon the plan sponsor's 401(k)/Company Retirement Plan. When you concentrate in a specific area (such as 401(k) or defined benefit or employee stock ownership plans) you should be the individual who is aware of what the plan sponsor needs. You, the Financial Advisor specialist, become the individual who makes sure that the plan sponsor intends to do their part to satisfy those needs. You should operate from your own checklist if you are a specialist within any one of the 401(k)/Company Retirement Plans. Not using a checklist is irresponsible. You should create a minimum set of standards from which all of your clients will benefit. (We understand that your internal restrictions may prohibit you from distributing non-approved checklists. That does not mean that you should ignore this altogether. Perhaps it becomes a verbal, rather than written, checklist between you and your client.)

You, better then anyone, should be in a position to know what the plan sponsor needs! And in most cases it is much different from glossy promotional materials, welcome letters or contractual documentation. Let's take some time and go through it.

It is the responsibility of the plan sponsor's legal counsel to ensure that all documentation is acceptable. Although the written law has a large impact on how 401(k)/Company Retirement Plans are managed, there is an equal portion of common sense that goes a long way in doing the right thing. Some plan sponsor's desires are the result of normal business management: time efficiency, resource efficiency and cost efficiency. All are reasonable.

Q. 144 *What are specific plan sponsor/client needs?*

To deliver the highest level of service possible you will need to exceed "everyday" service. Include in your checklist those topics and concepts which will help your plan sponsor/client. The following are needs that your plan sponsor/client should satisfy:

- ERISA Bond
- Documentation of 401(k) Vendor selection
- Fiduciary Review binder (or file), including:
  - Investment Policy Statement
  - Investment Policy Reviews
  - Plan and Trust Documents, including all amendments, addenda and attachments
  - Summary Plan Description, including all amendments, addenda and attachments
  - Statement of compliance with Regulation 404(c), including documents provided to employees
- Employee education curriculum
  - Group and one-on-one meetings
- Corporate goals for the plan to achieve

The items in this list can distinguish a good or adequate 401(k)/Company Retirement Plan from a great one! In many cases there is an implied assumption that "someone" has attended to these details and made sure that they are in place. There is often an element of blind trust on the part of the plan sponsor. You can truly separate yourself from the competition by creating your own checklist around these issues. Once again, your internal compliance department will have an opinion and may control what you can or cannot place in writing. Regardless of whether or not your firm permits you to provide your plan sponsor/client with a written list of these topics, make sure that your plan sponsor/client is fully aware of how important these topics are to the success of their plan.

Q. 145 *What needs to be coordinated for a successful 401(k)/Company Retirement Plan?*

Consider yourself the quarterback on the 401(k) relationship team. Your job is to facilitate employee education and communication. You should be available to meet with any and all interested parties, such as legal counsel, accountants, third-party administrators or consultants. Building strong 401(k)/Company Retirement Plan employee education and communication will increase your value in the eyes of the plan sponsor or the retirement committee.

Q. 146 *How much time should the plan sponsors spend on managing the plan?*

This answer is dependent upon the size of the asset base, the size of the company and the number of eligible employees. If properly designed and efficiently administered, the day to day internal workings of the sponsor's 401(k)/Company Retirement Plan should require no more than two to eight hours per week, provided that assets are less than $25 million. However, if you are operating in an antiquated environment, where paper is the recording medium of all transactions, you may see one part-time or full-time employee devoted to the plan under the $25 million threshold. For plans from $25 million – $50 million, at least one part-time employee is the norm.

Q. 147 *How much time should I spend educating the plan sponsor?*

Plan on spending at least two to four hours with the principal or entire retirement plan committee at the advent of any new 401(k)/Company Retirement Plan relationship. Remember, an educated plan sponsor is much simpler for you to communicate with and satisfy. Any relationship where one of the individuals is ignorant of the facts is frustrating. If your plan sponsor/client does not have a clear and accurate understanding of their own responsibility as well as more than a cursory understanding of your role in delivering service, you can anticipate lengthy conversations defending your actions. If you do not educate the plan sponsor and increase their awareness, someone else may — and you could suffer the consequences.

Q. 148 *What if the client or plan sponsor will not allocate the proper attention that a 401(k)/Company Retirement Plan requires?*

If the plan sponsor will not take the time to properly manage and allocate resources to the 401(k)/Company Retirement Plan, then you have a difficult decision to make. As a service provider to the plan sponsor and the 401(k)/Company Retirement Plan you have a responsibility to the plan participants. The extent of your liability will be determined by the documentation supporting the capacity in which you serve. If the plan sponsor does not want to have an optimum 401(k)/Company Retirement Plan, you may still be able to attain the results that you want from the plan for your business. The difficult decision that you and your team will be faced with is whether you choose to resign and fully disassociate yourself with the ongoing 401(k)/Company Retirement Plan or if you will elevate the plan sponsor's awareness to a higher level. There are many cases in which a Financial Advisor would have been better served by walking away from a bad (albeit profitable) client.

Q. 149 *What if I notice that the plan sponsor client has breached their fiduciary duty?*

Run (don't walk) to your supervisor or compliance officer or Office of Supervisory Jurisdiction. Report what you feel to be a fiduciary breach to your immediate supervisor. Each organization has its own internal procedure for addressing fiduciary breaches within client accounts. If you are exposed to such behavior it is your responsibility to immediately address any such breach in accordance with your internal policy. Looking the other way or doing nothing is not an option. As a fiduciary yourself (whether you are named or deemed) you have the responsibility to be aware of your duties.

Q. 150 *How do I convince the client to concentrate on those components that are important to the success of the plan?*

One effective method for elevating the plan sponsor's interest in properly managing their 401(k)/Company Retirement Plan is by sharing horror stories of those plan sponsors and individuals who have been sanctioned or criminally charged due to their negligence. If the consequences of managing a plan poorly or inappropriately will not get their attention, then chances are nothing will. Also, remind the plan sponsor of what they told you they wanted to accomplish with the 401(k)/Company Retirement Plan. If the plan sponsor wants the plan to enhance the productivity and profitability of the company then everything possible needs to be done to achieve that goal. A plan sponsor would not normally analyze and purchase a new computer system with the intent of making the employees as productive as possible, yet refuse to train the staff on how best to operate the new system. The employer would be making a similar mistake by neglecting to prudently manage and monitor the program provider and the components of the plan.

Q. 151 *What if the plan sponsor/client is not reviewing the correct information but they are relying on me (and are buying my product)?*

You have a big decision to make and you need to make the right one. If the plan sponsor is creating exposure for you in how they are handling their plan and your product, then you may need to resign. It is always better to educate the plan sponsor but just as in any educational environment you have students who will not accept or act upon knowledge. The exposure is too great for you to be associated with the plan when the plan sponsor is not taking their fiduciary duty seriously. Again, refer to the written or implied contractual requirements between you and your plan sponsor to obtain a full understanding of what you are obligated to provide or deliver. You should first attempt to educate the plan sponsor, by elevating their awareness around their fiduciary responsibility to monitor and evaluate services and service providers. Just because they are purchasing your product does not mean that they are an ideal 401(k)/Company Retirement Plan client.

Q. 152 *How do I respond if my client/prospect plan sponsor has no interest in managing the plan components?*

You are quite vulnerable when you are a partner with your client on their 401(k)/Company Retirement Plan. You have exposure to the client, the regulators and the plan participants. Many successful Financial Advisors have walked away from profitable business in order to preserve their reputation in this industry. If your client or prospect has no interest in prudently and efficiently managing their plan, you are best served by severing the relationship.

Q. 153 *How do I simplify 401(k)/Company Retirement Plan management for my client?*

One of the best tools available today is the Service Agreement. It sets forth in writing those areas of responsibility for both the plan sponsor and Financial Advisor. The Service Agreement is further developed in Appendix A.

Q. 154 *Where can I find fresh ideas?*

The best new ideas will usually come from your plan sponsor/clients and their plan participants. As stated earlier, you can obtain a wealth of information by simply asking your clients what they would like you to do. The voice of the customer is strong. Both employers and employees have ideas. The trick is to separate the truly good ones from the ordinary or absurd.

Other fresh ideas can come from industry wholesalers. Good whole-salers will always be available to help you grow your business. Make a point to utilize the expertise of a seasoned wholesaler to strengthen and solidify the relationship that you enjoy with each of your plan sponsors.

Another source of fresh ideas can come from outside of our industry. If you notice a particular process or system which is prevalent in manufacturing or information technology (or any other industry segment) do not be reluctant to adopt such a good practice into your business plan.

Section III – Continuous Improvement

10

Getting Better

An unwritten rule of continuous improvement is the acceptance of ongoing change. Anyone who intends to continuously improve must accept the fact that there will be ongoing change within the organization. As coaches we have frequently heard the comment "I want to double my business, make more money, have more time away from the office and have everything operate much smoother, but I don't really want to change anything that I'm doing." (Such a statement is the classic definition of "insanity" — continuing the same behavior and expecting different results.) This behavior can also manifest itself in the statement, "I know my process is as good as it can be, operationally we are rock solid — but I want to make more money and enjoy more free time."

Can you see the irony here? Every day many of us come into contact with "true insanity" in our business. In this industry you cannot expect to maintain old behavior patterns while simultaneously attaining new and improved results. It is just not that simple these days. Try to have some compassion for the individual who believes that results will be different by continuing old behaviors. They will surely suffer the consequences associated with that kind thinking.

If there was a single concept that captured the essence of this book, it would be "getting better." There are two distinct methodologies for improving processes. The first option is to make incremental adjustments to an existing process in pursuit of greater efficiency. (Think of it as taking your car in for a tune up.)

The alternative is to "re-engineer" the entire process or system. Instead of tweaking the existing system, discard it completely and replace it with a new one. In keeping with our car analogy, instead of taking your car in for a tune-up, you choose to purchase a new car.

When it comes to getting better there exist the same two options: fix what you have or replace what you have.

The Financial Advisor striving for Maximum Efficiency must continually have an honest, objective discussion with themselves after answering questions on Competition (Chapter 6), Retirement Plan Knowledge (Chapters 7 and 8), What the Client Wants (Chapter 9), Getting Better (this chapter), Process (Chapter 13) and Measurement (Chapter 18). You must ask yourself very difficult questions, answer them honestly and take action by formulating a plan around your weak components.

At the end of this chapter we will address four areas that pose great challenges to the majority of Financial Advisors who wish to take their business to the next level. We call those The Big Four because of their importance to every Financial Advisor on the path to improvement. Some consultants will read The Big Four and say "That's me! I must get better in that area!" There will be others who read The Big Four and shrug their shoulders, roll their eyes and shake their heads while saying "That's not me — NO way!" For those who believe that none of it applies to them we encourage them to review the earlier definition of insanity — continuing the same behavior and expecting different results.

We have included The Big Four — Prioritization, Communication, Time Management and Resource Allocation — due to the frequency with which they recur as challenges for Financial Advisors.

Q. 155 *How do I "get better"?*

You must first have the desire to get better. Without it your business will most likely go nowhere. You may be fortunate or you may be in the right place at the right time. You may even grow your business. However that is not necessarily improvement, but simply lucky circumstance. We do not believe it is prudent to count on good luck in planning the components of your success. Desire helps to build passion around what you do. Commit to doing those things that the majority of other Financial Advisors will not do — including proper research, working hard, properly utilizing all available resources (this could be thought of as working smart) and execution. If you wrap each of those components into your business in an efficient manner you should become much better at those functions you choose to perform.

Q. 156 *What questions should I ask myself if my goal is to get better?*

Address the most important aspects of success first. Do you have desire? Passion? Commitment? Work ethic? Proper utilization of assets? Flawless execution?

Be honest with yourself, and give a thoughtful answer to each of these questions.

 WRITE IT

Q. 157 *What else I can do in my efforts to get better?*

Self-analysis is your departure point for improving what you do. This should not be a one-time exercise but rather an ongoing process of regular examination and continuous evaluation. If you are truly serious about taking your business to the next level, then you must pose these continuous improvement questions to yourself at least every six months and preferably every quarter. Be willing to answer them objectively.

 WRITE IT

Q. 158 *Should I scrap my existing system and start over?*

If you believe that you can rehabilitate your broken or failing system to an acceptable level of efficiency by adjusting components of it, then you may be better served by keeping what you have and making improvements. Achieving improvement by tweaking your own internal processes and systems will normally be less expensive, less stressful from the standpoint of change management and will always be less disruptive. If you choose to make improvements to your existing system, keep in mind the intended outcome and make sure that your system is capable of delivering it after changes are made. Then set forth a plan comprised of incremental steps toward your intended outcome. If you believe that your existing system cannot be amended to the efficiency level desired, you are better served by replacing the system with an entirely new one.

> **Example** — *You are operating with a legacy database management system that is functional for generating direct mail and maintaining name, address, city, state and zip codes — however the existing system will not maintain current program provider or tickler information. The software company for this system makes a module that can be added for the vendor and tickler information. However no further upgrades are available or planned. Even with the new module the system is "maxed out." Obtaining the new module, customization, installation and education will consume approximately three to four months before the new database is fully operable.*

Your other option may be to replace the entire database management system with an off-the-shelf software package which could maintain all of the data that you intend to track. The new system should also be expandable to carry additional data with more functionality. The complete replacement of an old database system with a completely new one is more expensive, but your existing data can be exported to the new system and you can be fully functional in less than two weeks.

Improvement comes from either small steps or a complete overhaul!

— Self-assessment —

Q. 159 Where are you weak?

This is sometimes a very difficult question for a Financial Advisor. Generating production is quantitative in nature. Determining whether or not a quantitative goal has been met is simple. Some Financial Advisors (even those who are team leaders) have a mentality of, "as long as I meet my goals everything is acceptable." In reality, goals can be met in a dysfunctional environment. The question becomes, "How much better might our team have been or how much more rapidly might we have grown had we been operating together as a team?" It is important to look beyond the quantifiable aspects of your business and look at the soft skills with an eye toward making the team fully functional. This may include leadership (covered fully in Chapter 14), roles and responsibilities, setting strategy, establishing strategic partners or other areas.

 WRITE IT

Q. 160 Are those areas identified as weak currently targeted for improvement within your strategic objectives?

If not, consider a plan to improve upon these weaknesses.

Q. 161 Within the areas of presentation skills, setting strategy and lead generation, where are you the weakest?

If you or your team is weak within any of these three areas, then your attempt to successfully grow your 401(k)/Company Retirement Plan business will be stymied! Every aspect of running your business is important; however each of these three areas can greatly impact your success. We asked specifically about these areas because it is sometimes difficult for a Financial Advisor or the leader of a financial service's team to come to grips with shortcomings in these three areas.

 WRITE IT

Q. 162 Do you have sufficient knowledge within this industry to help plan sponsors?

You will need to do a bit of research to get the answer to this one. We suggest that you solicit some of your current clients, some of your prospects and some of your former clients. Such a cross section of objective plan sponsors should give you a reasonable understanding of how you are perceived in the marketplace. Make a note of those you will call to obtain this information.

 WRITE IT

Q. 163 **Are you targeting a market where your skills and knowledge base are deficient?**

Do not attempt to grow your business in the $100 million market if your knowledge base is incapable of meeting the expectations of a plan sponsor at that level. It is imperative that your skill level match the expectations of the plan sponsors with whom you interact.

Q. 164 *What areas should be identified and targeted first for improvement within a financial services team?*

Every financial services team is different — not necessarily unique, but different. Since there are some similarities among financial service teams and their Financial Advisors, there are specific areas we usually attempt to strengthen first. We refer to these areas as The Big Four:

- Prioritization
- Communication
- Time management
- Resource allocation

We look to these areas first since incremental improvements in any one of them will immediately return big dividends to the team. Every time your team achieves an improvement in Prioritization, Communications, Time Management or Resource Allocation — your team becomes stronger and more efficient! The Big Four serve as the infrastructure to your business.

Q. 165 *Would I benefit from utilizing an outside resource for evaluating my capabilities?*

Although it is not required for continuous improvement, most Financial Advisors would greatly benefit by having an objective set of eyes observe their operation, behavior and outcomes. (There are some Financial Advisors in the marketplace who feel that they are "as good as they can be." We can guarantee the accuracy of that statement as its own self-fulfilling prophecy.)

There are teams who are capable of continuous improvement without the direction of outside assistance. Those teams and Financial Advisors are the exception rather than the rule.

Q. 166 *Prioritization has always been challenging for me. What tips can you provide so that I can effectively prioritize my tasks as well as those of my team?*

Each Financial Advisor or financial service team will have established their own set of priorities in order to accomplish their Vision. (Remember, if a specific task does not assist you in achieving your Business Plan or strategic objectives, then you must question whether the task is worth your time to complete.) In the absence of a documented Business Plan, prioritization becomes guesswork. Since the Business Plan states what needs to be done (including who is responsible for each specific task) and provides a beginning and ending or due date, most of your prioritization will have been completed during its documentation. The Business Plan and the Strategic Plan are your keys to prioritization. Without either of these guiding and directing your day-to-day activities, you will be guessing.

A good check for the effectiveness of your prioritization would be to maintain a daily log for a period of one week. At the end of the week, look back at the log. Take note of how much of your week was spent on activities which were building for the future versus how much of your week was spent on fixing problems, putting out fires or managing people. If you have a question of prioritization, the daily log is an effective exercise and serves as a good reference point for future improvement. For even better results, maintain the daily log for 30 days. Then review the data. After you see where your time is being spent, you may decide to re-prioritize your tasks.

Q. 167   *How do I improve communication with my team or group?*

Any successful team must communicate on a regular basis. Hold regular meetings at least once a week. This may feel awkward at first, especially in a small group of two or three, but you will quickly learn that the benefits outweigh any concerns. Do not let anything keep you from holding these very important meetings; skipping them is counterproductive. In between weekly meetings, communicate with your team as often as necessary with person-to-person conversations, e-mails and memos. Do not ever let your clients have the impression that "the right hand doesn't know what the left hand is doing."

Q. 168   *We are a small group of three — two producers and one administrative assistant. What kind of meeting would we hold?*

Regardless of the size of your group, meetings should be held regularly and scheduled in advance. A weekly one-hour meeting scheduled every Tuesday at 9 a.m. or every Thursday at 4 p.m. (or any date and time) will provide your team with an opportunity to exchange ideas and check the status of ongoing projects in an uninterrupted environment. These meetings do not need to last any longer than they are productive. If you feel you will not have enough content for a one-hour meeting, that is fine. Schedule your meeting for 20 or 30 minutes. No one is disappointed when a meeting ends early. The shorter the team meeting, the better! The structure here is just as important as the content. As the team leader you should be included in everything that has an impact on the team. The regularity of the team meeting instills confidence and a feeling of inclusion in those team members who would not normally be privy to your day-to-day ideas and decisions.

All meetings must include:

- A printed agenda which includes a purpose and the objectives; the agenda should also include the location, date, both beginning and ending time, the individuals attending and their respective responsibilities/assignments.
- A scribe or recorder assigned to the meeting for note taking and documentation purposes.

- A summary of key issues.
- An action plan for each agenda topic; assign an individual to be responsible for accomplishing each key point (issue or task), provide an estimated timeline for completion of that point and establish a timeline for reporting back to the group.

Q. 169 *Time management seems to be a challenge for me. How can I better utilize the time that I spend developing 401(k) / Company Retirement Plan business?*

Some of the following suggestions may seem extreme. But when you observe the behaviors and daily patterns of successful Financial Advisors you will find that they are extraordinarily judicious in the management of their time. Here are some quick suggestions for maximizing your time:

- Avoid incoming telephone interruptions (with the exception of true emergencies).
- Institute "quiet time" parameters (periods of the day when work can be done without interruption).
- Limit conversations:
  - The number
  - The duration
  - The topics
- Install a procedure for placing outgoing calls:
  - Three- to five-minute time limit
  - Utilize voicemail to its fullest
  - Limit "chit chat"

When initiating conversations with individuals who have a history of remaining on the line too long, we suggest that you begin with the statement, "I have a very busy day today but I felt it quite important to take five minutes to contact you." Doing so will reinforce how important the call is to you but at the same time it should send a signal to the other party that you are not in a position to be on the phone for a long time.

If you use a cell phone during travel, take some time before you depart (whether for a short drive or an overnight trip) to organize the calls that you will be making from the road. If you feel that you can safely conduct business while traveling, this is an excellent opportunity to maximize efficiencies during what would normally be downtime.

Q. 170 *I struggle with resource allocation. I have a diffi-*
cult time discerning if I have fully utilized the
resources available to me and my team. How do I
best allocate resources for maximum productivity?

Resource allocation will be dramatically different for everyone. Every Financial Advisor and financial services team has a unique set of resources available. There are a variety of reasons why resources may have been underutilized. Many Financial Advisors do not have an accurate understanding of what resources are available to them within the firm. Another cause of underutilization of resources is a lack of knowledge or education as it pertains to a particular resource. (For example, you may possess the latest technology for producing high-quality, informative and visually appealing client reports, however without the understanding of how those reports can be produced, that technology is worthless to you and your team — underutilization!)

It should be obvious that it is impossible to properly allocate resources if you do not know what resources are available to you. Or if you know what resources are available, but do not have the knowledge to operate the tools, then you again have the case of an under-utilized resource — or improper resource allocation. Assuming you possess a full awareness of available resources and the full capability of operating those resources, your challenge now becomes one of utilization and allocation.

Resources can be software programs, hard-copy printed materials, individuals or any other "tool" which helps you deliver products or services to your clients. The non-human assets would fall into one category of resource. The other category, human assets (those individuals who are part of your financial services team) are a dynamic resource available to you. Your team needs to utilize the human capital of the firm to the fullest capacity. At this point you want to discover human capital resources that have been underutilized or have excess capacity. Put another way, who on your team is sitting and watching others work? Could that person help the team accomplish more? What would that require? Do they need training, motivation or a pink slip?

The outline for resource allocation is:

- Take inventory of available resources
- Analyze utilization (is there unused capacity?)
- Revise the resource, re-allocate the resource or re-train the team

How you work with human capital (your financial services team) will be different than how you re-allocate equipment, however the methodology that you utilize for properly allocating the resources will be the same.

11

Professional Development

Just as your business grows in the 401(k)/Company Retirement Plan marketplace, so does your need to effectively increase service levels to your institutional and individual clients. Concurrently you should continue to develop your abilities relating to technical and professional expertise.

One of the benefits of being a Financial Advisor is the freedom that you enjoy being able to control your own developmental path. Some of the areas which you may choose to develop include management, leadership, sales, technical, legal or accounting. You can be highly focused on any one of these areas. Hopefully you will become a better decision maker as a result of your developmental efforts.

Professional development should be a well-thought-out process.

You (and your clients) are best served if you take control of your career development and that of your team. Professional development takes time, but it is worth every minute. It should always be thought of as working toward a goal. Your own development may focus on management, leadership or strategy whereas members of your team should be focused on improving individual components such as customer service, telephone etiquette or time management.

When structuring professional development for your team members, consider utilizing the outside training and development effort as a reward for a job well done. Doing so creates a substantial return on investment for everyone — including your plan sponsor clients!

Q. 171 *How do I keep an edge over the competition?*

You can maintain your edge by being a member of and participating in industry organizations, by attending conferences and seminars and by pursuing higher-level designations. Doing so will ensure that you are always current with the latest standards, processes, systems and technology. You must also be willing to work hard at the same time you are working smart.

Q. 172 **Which industry related professional organizations do you belong to?**

This is an excellent starting point for taking inventory of your professional credentials. The firm with which you are affiliated as well as the organizations of which you are a member define "who you are" as a professional in the marketplace. Assuming that you have all of the professional training and education offered through those organizations to which you belong, are you qualified to service a 401(k)/Company Retirement Plan? Take a moment to itemize the training offered by your membership organizations. We advise that you maintain your competitive edge by being a member of and participating in industry organizations.

 WRITE IT

Q. 173 *What associations would I benefit by joining?*

- American Society of Pension Professionals and Actuaries (ASPPA)
- Employee Benefit Research Institute (EBRI)
- International Foundation Education Benefits Compensation (IFEBC)
- Profit Sharing Council of America (PSCA)

Q. 174 Which local and national non-professional organizations do you belong to?

Do your current non-professional memberships satisfy your personal goals and civic interests?

 WRITE IT

Q. 175 Are you planning to attend any "topic specific" seminars?

Seminars are an excellent use of time for gaining targeted knowledge and awareness of a specific topic. Usually seminars will be single-focus and short-duration sessions that will elevate your expertise in a specific area. Before you register for any seminar it makes sense to review the list of speakers so that you can be confident that the material and presentations will be worth your time and money.

 WRITE IT

Q. 176 Are you planning to attend any national conferences?

Conferences provide broad exposure to a segment of an industry and can also serve as valuable networking experiences. Conferences are more of a "shotgun-approach" to learning. Conferences will usually have concurrent sessions and general sessions. Before deciding to attend a conference, make sure that you can attend a sufficient number of sessions to make the overall conference a good value for your time and money. Do not underestimate the value of being in the same room as your competitors and meeting them. At many conferences, what you learn from your peers may exceed what you learn from the presenters. Having a peer contact in your industry but not in your marketplace is an extremely valuable asset.

 WRITE IT

Q. 177 *Is it important to obtain professional designations?*

We believe it is. However, a challenge for every Financial Advisor today is weeding through the thicket of available designations. There are many that might be a good fit for your business and the 401(k)/ Company Retirement Plan clients you serve.

Q. 178 *What designations are respected in our industry?*

This would be a very simple question for us to answer if it were not for copyright and trademark concerns. They are many designations available to the Financial Advisor who intends to grow their business in the 401(k)/Company Retirement Plan arena. A challenge for us, the authors, is the manner in which we print and reference the various designations to the reader. We have chosen to furnish you with a list of web sites where various retirement plan industry specific designations are available. To follow are the web sites of those firms that offer industry designations:

www.plansponsor.com	Designation and information
www.fi360.com	Designations and fiduciary training
www.asppa.org	Designations and training
www.cfp.net	Designation
www.ifebp.org	Designations and training
www.imca.org/certify	Designation
www.cfainstitute.org	Designation
www.cannonfinancial.com	Designations and training

Q. 179 **What designations do you think you should obtain in the next one to three years?**

Are there industry designations that you feel you lack? Have you analyzed the designations held by your toughest competitors? You should know what designations your competitors possess. After you have learned of your competitors' designations you will need to decide which of those designations are valuable to your business and if the designation is within your reach.

 WRITE IT

Q. 180 What continuing education requirements must you satisfy based upon your current professional designations or state and national registrations?

With a little research you may find that some of your continuing education requirements can be satisfied by your pursuit of additional professional designations. Some research on the front end will provide you with what you need to pursue such designations.

 WRITE IT

Q. 181 What is your plan to promote your marketplace knowledge?

It makes sense to share with your clients and prospects what new designations you have received. It is an excellent avenue for remaining in contact with plan sponsors in a positive way.

 WRITE IT

Q. 182 What resources do you use to stay current with the employer-sponsored savings plan?

There are "direct" and "pass-through" resources. "Direct" resources for marketplace information are The Department of Labor type of information repositories. Other examples include information published by the SEC and NASD. "Pass-through" resources are industry periodicals and all electronic marketing means. Another would be 401(k)/Company Retirement Plan program provider wholesalers. All are great. From where are you obtaining your marketplace intelligence?

 WRITE IT

General industry and targeted information is available at the following web sites:

www.401khelpcenter.com	Information
www.horsesmouth.com	Information
www.401kwire.com	Information
www.tag.com	Information

Participant support services can be found at the following web sites:

www.newkirk.com	Participant
www.investmenthorizons.com	Participant

Additional industry web sites:

www.psca.org	Organization
www.ebri.org	Organization
www.asppa.org	Organization

You will notice a substantial amount of overlap among the products and services offered by the firms represented above. If a web site is listed in a particular section, it does not mean that their product and service offerings are restricted to that listing. It only indicates that the web site firm is a recognized provider of such products and services. There are a multitude of firms and organizations that service the industry but have not been mentioned above. We performed a web-search of "401(k) service providers" that yielded approximately 400,000 other firms. Those mentioned above are perceived to have a national presence and should be readily available to Financial Advisors throughout the United States.

Q. 183 What actions will you be taking for professional development, designations, conferences, etc.

If you have not already done so, plan your professional development strategy now. List improvements you will make to your skill sets over the next one- to three-year period. Time and money will enter into your decision regarding the resources you can commit. However, ignoring professional development completely will undoubtedly cost you future plan sponsor/clients.

 WRITE IT

12

Developing
Strategic Partners

Strategic partnering is joining with another Financial Advisor or forming a network with other industry professionals such as third-party
administrators, CPAs, non-competing search consultants, program
provider wholesalers and ERISA attorneys. Strategic partners work
together to pursue a 401(k)/Company Retirement Plan prospect in the
hope of attaining them as a client and, if applicable, share revenue
and or service responsibilities on an ongoing basis.

Each strategic partner, (including you) contributes to enhance the
probability of acquisition and retention of the plan. Additionally,
strategic partners are capable of reciprocating and bringing to you
opportunities that they discover. Remember, you may have to work
with industry professionals who not only deliver their discipline but
also are securities licensed. Form your network of strategic partners
with professionals who do not want to encroach on your revenue
opportunities. There may be some overlap in the products or services
offered by your strategic partners, but healthy partnerships are win-
win situations.

The purpose of forming a strategic partnership is that by teaming
you will increase your probability of attaining the 401(k)/Company
Retirement Plan versus going it alone. Typically you might team with
a strategic partner who has a stronger relationship with the decision
maker at a company who has a plan that you would like to acquire.

Q. 184   *Who might be my strategic partners?*

Strategic partners can include peer Financial Advisors or other financial sales professionals who do not deliver products which might compete with the 401(k)/Company Retirement Plans. For example, insurance professionals who specialize in property and casualty or health can become excellent strategic partners for Financial Advisors who specialize in 401(k)/Company Retirement Plan markets.

Q. 185   *Should I build my business alone or seek the assistance of others, either as strategic partners or team members?*

You may need a stronger "political" presence than you can project alone. Or perhaps you are weak in a particular area. Strategic partners can help "fill in your gaps." More than anything, they may help you to acquire business that you might not have had access to on your own. If you do form a strategic partnership, then do so with the foundation of a Strategic Partnership Agreement (described later in this chapter).

Q. 186   *What industry professional classifications should I consider including in my strategic partnership network and how can we work together?*

Financial Advisor — You may want to form a strategic partnership with a peer Financial Advisor because they have strong relationships with decision maker(s) at companies who have 401(k)/Company Retirement Plans that you find attractive. Whether they are peer Financial Advisors in your branch complex or around the nation, peer or unaffiliated Financial Advisors in your community or around the nation, strategic partners can assist you in landing a 401(k)/Company Retirement Plan in which you may need a stronger "political" presence than you have alone. By forming a strategic partnership with a peer Financial Advisor, you can leverage their relationships and they can have confidence that their client is going to be taken care of by you. Your strategic partner can win in two ways:

• The relationship they have with their clients is strengthened as a result of their leadership in forming a strategic alliance with you.

- They can receive compensation without major tactical responsibilities of plan conversion management or ongoing employee education.

Benefit Broker — These professionals may serve the spectrum of employee benefit programs. Ideally you should search for benefit brokers that offer all benefits other than 401(k)/Company Retirement Plans. They have relationships that they can refer you to, and you in turn can refer them to your 401(k)/Company Retirement Plan clients who need assistance with other employee benefit programs such as health, dental or executive compensation.

Third-Party Administrators (TPAs) — TPAs can provide the technical expertise to ensure that your plan sponsor has the best plan design for achieving their objectives. They also provide ongoing plan administration and consulting to make sure that a complicated plan operates at an optimal level. TPAs typically are not exceptional marketers or sales people.

Certified Public Accountants (CPAs) — 401(k)/Company Retirement Plans that exceed 100 eligible employees require an annual audit. This is a function that CPAs can complete. Additionally, CPAs can have social and business relationships with decision makers. In the small- and mid-size 401(k)/Company Retirement Plan marketplace, CPAs serve a strategic role as provider of business services and consulting. CPAs who work closely with decision makers for their individual needs or with their company will not want to be excluded from meetings that you conduct with their clients.

Search Consultant — Plan sponsors hire search consultants for general 401(k)/Company Retirement Plan advice. Their responsibilities might also involve monitoring program providers and/or components (investments, etc.) of the plan. Recommending that a plan sponsor employ a search consultant can ensure that you compete for a 401(k)/Company Retirement Plan on a level playing field. Search consultants can be in a position to invite you to participate in searches of which you otherwise may not have been aware.

Program Provider Wholesaler — Program provider wholesalers are compensated to close 401(k)/Company Retirement Plan business through intermediaries. They seek to be active in the sales process to increase the probability of their firm's program being chosen by both a Financial Advisor and the plan sponsor. They therefore want to partner with competent Financial Advisors who can deliver high quality service and support. Also, they could "flip" to you "orphan plans" — 401(k)/Company Retirement Plans without an assigned Financial Advisor.

ERISA Attorney — ERISA attorneys contribute to the awareness that plan sponsors have concerning their fiduciary responsibilities and the process of managing them. They are the experts in ERISA — not you! Top ERISA attorneys will recognize your great value and recommend you to their plan sponsor clients. ERISA attorneys typically are not good marketers or sales people.

Q. 187 *Besides the direct involvement of a sale to a plan prospect, what are other ways to develop my strategic partnership network?*

Study Groups — Share current topics/discussion points relevant to each network member's discipline. Have scheduled meetings where each group member shares information concerning their specific interest. Dialogue ensues as each group member quizzes the presenter and shares in a roundtable discussion to strengthen all members' understanding as to how the topic impacts their discipline, their clients and their prospects.

Sales Network — Trust is the foundation of relationships. Industry professionals want to refer their clients to those whom they trust to do the right thing for them.

Set up quarterly breakfast or lunch presentations where network members invite their clients to hear from each member on changes within their specific area of expertise.

Q. 188 How many strategic partners do you currently work with?

When responding to this question, take some time to formulate your answer. The question is referencing true strategic partners, versus how many "people" or "entities" with whom you work. Remember a strategic partner is an organization that you have identified, targeted and sought out in an effort to make your deliverable to your client as good as it can be! Your strategic partnership could also be the result of the partner identifying, targeting and seeking your firm. So, how many?

 WRITE IT

Q. 189 How long have you been working with your current strategic partners?

Are your partnerships established or are they in the embryonic stage? The longer the partnership has been in place the simpler it is for you to evaluate the effectiveness and the benefits of the relationship.

 WRITE IT

Q. 190 Where do you (your organization or you as an individual) add value to your strategic partners?

You should have a clear understanding of what you bring to the table. If you can not quickly verbalize in a few sentences how you are benefiting your strategic partner as well as the 401(k)/Company Retirement Plan client, then perhaps your strategic partner is beginning to wonder why they should continue working with you.

 WRITE IT

Q. 191   *What if I notice that my competition appears to have strategic partnerships that I am missing and I have not developed?*

If you see this is the case, you will want to conduct some analysis on whether or not you are truly missing a strategic partner or if you are actually providing better service without employing a strategic partner. If you are not providing the same level of service as your competition, you must then determine which strategic partners best fit your needs to bring your service level to the point where it places you at least "on par" with the competition.

Q. 192   *Should I be looking at developing new strategic partners?*

You should always be open to adding new strategic partners. Your Business Plan should give your team direction on which strategic partners you should develop; however always keep your eyes open for the next opportunity.

Q. 193   *Why use a Strategic Partnership Agreement?*

Use a written agreement with your strategic partners — especially when you share revenue and specific responsibilities — so that everyone has a common understanding of roles, process, goals, revenue sharing and termination procedures if applicable. Written agreements create the clarity essential for a good relationship, allowing each partner to focus on the special skills they bring to the table. An agreement may not be necessary when your strategic partner simply refers business to you with no expectation of compensation.

Q. 194   *What are the components of a Strategic Partnership Agreement?*

Statement of Purpose — The Statement of Purpose describes why you and your strategic partner are entering into the strategic partnership.

Example of Strategic Partnership Agreement between Financial Advisors

(Name of your team or your name) and our strategic partner ((name[s]) will assist (city/territory) area based employers with maximizing the benefits of an effective 401(k) plan. We will harness the global resources of (broker dealer/program provider) along with the abilities of the Retirement Plan Group at ABC Company to achieve our purpose. We believe that relationships are very important in acquiring and retaining 401(k) plans. We have great respect for the personal and professional relationships our strategic partner (name[s]) have with key decision makers at our target companies. We believe that a core competency of (name of your team or your name) is serving the retirement plan needs of (city/territory) area employers. Combining the great value of our strategic partner (name[s]) relationships with our core competency will provide for successful acquisition and retention of 401(k) plans.

The Roles and Process — Defining both the roles for each participant in the strategic partnership as well as the process that all partners will adhere to will ensure that you and all of your partners will effectively employ your respective energies to achieve the intended outcomes.

Example:
- *SP #1 will be responsible for developing the list of prospects.*
- *SP #2 will review the prospect list identifying those prospects where SP #2 has an existing relationship.*
- *SP #1 and SP #2 will then prepare a joint letter to be sent to those prospects identified by SP #2 that introduces the alliance and asks for the opportunity to meet.*

Goals — What are the goals you want to achieve with your strategic partner? Be specific in defining your goals.

Example: *We will acquire 20 401(k) plans, representing $200,000,000 in assets over the next five years.*

Revenue Sharing — You can remain confident that this is the number-one item you will negotiate with your strategic partner, if applicable. However revenue is derived, it should be spelled out, as well as how the revenue will be distributed among all partners.

> **Example:** *All gross production credits received from the 401(k) plan will be split perpetually 70% to (name of your team or your name) and 30% to the strategic partner (name[s]). Additionally, strategic partner (name[s]) will retain the relationships and any cross-selling opportunities with the decision makers and other employees that they define prior to winning the 401(k) plan. Any future related business awarded by the client company where the expertise of (name of your team or your name) is retained is to be split perpetually 70% to (name of your team or your name) and 30% to strategic partner (name[s]). (Name of your team or your name) will publish a compensation report quarterly to strategic partner (name[s]).*

Termination procedures — A "pre-nuptial" type agreement is a prudent step for your partnership to take. It is best to decide how the client relationship would be handled in the event of dissolution of the strategic partnership. This is better done when establishing the partnership rather than in the heat of "divorce," no matter how amicable.

> **Example:** *In the event of termination of the strategic partnership, the shared business will be split in a fashion that is considered "fair and equitable" by an arbitration panel of up to three individuals. One member of the panel will be chosen by (name), another by the strategic partner Financial Advisor and one member by the office manager.*

> *Signatures and Date of Agreement:* (There is no better way to prove your commitment to the partnership than by applying your name to the Agreement.)

_____

(Name of your team or your name)

_____

(Name(s) of strategic partner)

Date _____

Q. 195 *Should strategic partners be involved in the sales cycle?*

Yes. We encourage all strategic partners to take an active role throughout the 401(k)/Company Retirement Plan sales cycle. However we realize that you, as the Financial Advisor, should lead the charge in defining and executing all acquisition and retention activities, including:

- Prospecting
- Profiling
- Presentations
- Service implementation
- Ongoing service

Q. 196 *Should I be evaluating my strategic partners and our partnership arrangement on an ongoing basis?*

Yes, you absolutely should evaluate every one of your strategic partners at least annually. Review the partnership for effectiveness, service quality, profitability and results versus goals as established within the Strategic Partnership Agreement.

13

Process

One of the greatest obstacles facing our industry today is that most Financial Advisors do not understand that what they deliver is a series of processes to both their client and to their employer.

Many of the plan sponsor/clients that you serve will have a strong background in process management. This is not the case for the majority of Financial Advisors serving those plan sponsors. Most of today's Financial Advisors have no more than a cursory understanding of process management or related topics such as Total Quality Management, Lean Processing or Six Sigma.

The strong process management background of the plan sponsors' executive team will cause them to study you, the processes you perform and the systems that you utilize a little differently then you might anticipate. While you might be single-focused on the end result — for the benefit of all plan participants — your plan sponsors' executive teams are most likely noticing, and in some cases analyzing, the processes you utilize in managing their account. These very astute executive teams are also taking notice of how you manage your own business.

As a business, your plan sponsor clients will either thrive or survive. The difference between a thriving business and a surviving business can be their processes alone. When competing companies begin with the same raw materials and fabricate a similar product, why would one company succeed while the other fails? All work is a series of processes, which some companies perform well and others perform poorly.

Even the giants within an industry cannot survive without sound processes. Consider what has occurred globally in the automotive industry over the past two decades. Our once world-leading automotive companies resisted change and adhered to their existing poor processes. They were unseated by smaller up-and-coming firms while they continued to deliver an inferior product. All of these firms began with the same raw materials. The major difference between the thriving automotive companies and those that are floundering is their processes.

This is an oversimplification, but it is not an exaggeration.

Financial Advisors who are process-oriented spend very little, if any, time and resources fixing things that are wrong or in fighting fires within their own organization. Executing processes flawlessly will greatly reduce, and hopefully eliminate, waste in your organization. This is the reason that your clients will be monitoring your business practices. They want to be sure that they are not paying for your mistakes. Financial Advisors who position their resources to satisfy (or exceed) customer requirements — every time — will be process oriented teams that achieve their Vision.

This chapter will not attempt to transform every reader into a Six Sigma Black Belt or a Lean Manufacturing Guru but we will strive to make every reader comfortable with just a few of the processes associated with successful 401(k)/Company Retirement Plan management.

Q. 197   Do you have a clear understanding that all work is a process to be performed or conducted?

For those of you who might feel that financial advising is different from making widgets — you're right! It *is* different. However, many highly successful organizations know that all work is a series of processes. As your team develops there is a greater need for you to understand the processes involved in managing your business.

Q. 198   Do you manage your business as a series of processes or does your organization operate by addressing which fire needs to be extinguished next?

If you spend more time putting out fires than you spend planning for the future, we would guess that strong and established processes do not exist within your team. If that is the case, you are not nearly as efficient as you can become.

 WRITE IT

Q. 199 Can you describe your current processes for acquiring new 401(k)/Company Retirement Plan business?

If you do not have a clear process for the development of new business, then you must change that! Process is what will enable you to repeat your successful past practices. Process delivers the efficiency of an assembly-line to the very personal components of your business.

Most sales training organizations will provide you with a process that will assist you in your effort to acquire new business.

 WRITE IT

Q. 200 *What would a plan acquisition process look like?*

A sample plan acquisition process-system could look like this:

Identify ➤ Target ➤ Discovery ➤ Proposal ➤ Close ➤ Client

The above process system will not be appropriate for everyone. It is most important that you develop a process that will satisfy your requirements, satisfy the client requirements and deliver to you (or your team) the outcomes that you desire.

An acquisition process that includes a strategic partner can be outlined in this way:

Sample Process for: Account Acquisition

- *(Name of your team or your name)* will provide *(name[s] of strategic partner[s])* a list of 200 *(location)* area target 401(k) plans. Each plan will have a minimum of $4 million in plan assets and less than 1000 employees.

- *(Name[s] of strategic partner)* will identify those plans with which they have a relationship with a key decision maker.
- *(Name of your team or your name)* will then provide detailed data on the plan(s) identified and coach *(name[s] of strategic partner[s])* as to the selling points regarding the target 401(k) plan.
- *(Name[s]) of strategic partner[s])* will then contact the key decision maker at the target plan(s) and arrange a meeting with the decision maker(s) of the target 401(k) plan themselves and *(name of your team or your name)*.
- *(Name of your team or your name)* will be responsible for the prospecting, profiling, proposal and sales presentation processes, while *(name[s] of strategic partner[s])* stays continually involved and provides assistance in managing the relationship.
- *(Name of your team or your name)* will report to *(name(s) of strategic partner[s])* throughout the retention phase with the target 401(k)/Company Retirement Plan.

Q. 201   Can you describe your current processes for retaining your existing 401(k)/Company Retirement Plan business?

It is vitally important that you have a process for the retention and servicing of your clients. If you utilize a Service Agreement then you have in all likelihood satisfied the requirement of having a process for retaining your clients. Processes must be repeatable. Whatever your process is for retaining business you should be able to execute it flawlessly.

 WRITE IT

Q. 202   *What would a plan retention process look like?*

Sample Process for: Account Retention
- Once the target 401(k) plan is acquired, *(name of your team or your name)* will conduct all necessary implementation and ongoing service processes, including:
    - Coordination of all operational events including plan document design, transfer of plan data and initial communication to employees.

- Development of an Investment Policy Statement (IPS) detailing guidelines for selecting and removing funds. In addition we will provide quarterly reviews and monitoring of each fund in the plan.
- Development and delivery of an employee education curriculum designed to fit the needs of all employees.
- Annual trustee meeting and assistance with the management of their fiduciary responsibilities including review of the Department of Labor 401(k) Plan Fee Disclosure Form, Investment Policy Statement and Employee Education Initiatives.

Q. 203 *Can you give an example of a decision making process?*

Let's say you need to decide whether or not to invest in the latest technology for managing your business. Break it down into a series of questions, always keeping in mind your Business Plan and Strategic Plan. For instance:

1) Can I or an associate run the system (not just according to the vendor or the sales material but if I have to use the system, can I make it work)?

 WRITE IT

2) Will using the new system enhance my efforts (put another way, will it help me achieve my Strategic Plan and ultimately my Vision)?

 WRITE IT

3) If properly expensed or amortized, will the new system deliver value greater than the total expense associated with the product? (The total expense would include the entire capital expenditure,

the amount of time required to learn the new system by the system operator, and the amount of time it takes to efficiently run and utilize the system.)

WRITE IT

The answers to the questions that you have created for yourself will help you make your decision. In this case, if any of your answers are "no," then you should not invest in that particular technology.

Section IV –
Your
Responsibility

14

Leadership and Strategy

Every team needs a leader. As the leader of your team you will be charged with guiding everyone to the Vision. There are a variety of opinions on what constitutes leadership. Is one type of leadership style the very best or can any style work if applied properly by the leader? Regardless of how you answer this question, there are identifiable traits that most successful leaders frequently exhibit.

Successful leadership requires the clear expression of a common goal for the team. True leadership is about the execution of a well-defined and clearly communicated strategy. Leaders can rise to their leadership role by virtue of being appointed, assuming the role themselves or by being selected by the rest of the team. Both leader and the led must be committed to the Vision. Successful leaders will demonstrate a conviction to the cause, an unwavering courage to deliver results, a strong ability to communicate with subordinates and a clear focus on the strategy to be employed. True leaders set aside ego and concentrate on what is required to reach the goal.

The leader is responsible for outlining the strategy to the entire team. The team will follow and carry out the wishes of the leader only if the members of the team perceive that the Vision is worth the effort and that the leader is capable of guiding them to it.

There is a large component of change management associated with any leadership role. You may need to develop a start-up marketing plan, realign your sales effort or re-assign human capital to improve operational functions of your business. Unless you intend to scrap every system and resource available to you and build fresh from the ground up, each of these described improvements presents a change management challenge. Successful change management requires strong leadership! To scrap old systems and buy new requires time and capital. A strong leader possesses a keen eye for diagnosing a situation. Options available for improving performance are limited. As the leader of your team, you must have the ability to identify the appropriate response to every situation, be it:

• Starting fresh
• A turnaround situation
• Re-aligning existing resources
• Maintaining the status quo

Setting strategy (after determining the proper course among the four options above) will be the preliminary step in effecting successful change management. Within any successful change management effort, setting the strategy is crucial. As a leader you must prepare those around you to embrace disruption. The leader must convey to the team that the future disruption will result in the building of a much stronger team that will be better positioned for accomplishing the organizational goals.

Many leaders make the mistake of not effectively communicating that there will be disruption and distraction along the way. You should not expect your team to participate in or become excited about change if you have not made it clear what is expected from each of them. There can be a number of negative responses to change — resistance, immobilization, fear, anger, depression, etc. One of your tasks as leader is to anticipate when members of the team will be second-guessing leadership and the effort.

If you are truly interested in making your team better, then you should seriously consider:

• Your ability to lead
• Your leadership style
• Your team's belief in your ability to lead
• Your team's ability to change
• Your ability to accurately assess what needs to be done

Setting strategy includes planning and plotting the course. Leaders must understand and comprehend the market and the team's ability to serve that market. You must understand the positioning of your product or service, especially as it relates to the competition. Strategic thinking requires an ability to connect the present with your Vision. As the team leader and the strategic thinker for your group, a large part of your time should be spent looking two to four steps "down the road" (if not you, then who?) Understand that not everyone on your team has the ability to think strategically. Consider such ability to be an art. If you are a team leader, we suggest that you have a strategy session approximately every 12 to 24 months. If you are not proficient in thinking strategically, you may want to consider outside assistance. We suggest that you can significantly collapse the learning curve for strategic thinking by using an outside resource to deliver a strategic-thinking workshop or session to your leadership team.

Q. 204 What is your leadership style?

To best utilize your talents as a leader you must be aware of how you are perceived by your team. Is your leadership style assertive, driven, analytical, a facilitator or another? Each of these leadership styles sends a different message and will be received differently by members of your team. In most cases any style will work as long as you are consistent.

Q. 205 *Does a team of one need a leader?*

Even though you may be a sole Financial Advisor, you still need to operate within a structured arrangement if you want to prosper and grow. Most likely you will work with an assistant or a lead generator. Usually there is at least one other person. Even if you are performing many of the tasks yourself, your associates still need direction. There must be someone who can analyze a situation, make a decision and lead its execution. As leader, that is your job.

Team Approach

Q. 206 *How do we choose a leader for our team?*

Frequently a logical, natural leader will emerge. The leader of the team should be someone who shares the Vision and has the confidence and support of the team. The team must believe that the leader is the right person to guide them to the destination — the Vision.

Q. 207 *What is the most common mistake made by Financial Advisor team leaders?*

The most common mistake is not regarding leadership as their number-one priority. Many times a team leader will fall back into the role of producer (a comfortable role for many) at the expense of leading the team. If you are truly trying to build a team structure, backsliding to a producer role will adversely impact your team's ability to achieve the intended results.

Q. 208 *What are the potential pitfalls of a Financial Advisor assuming the role of team leader?*

There are primarily two areas of concern when a Financial Advisor assumes team leadership:

- The individual may not possess leadership qualities
- The team does not respect or recognize the authority of the newly appointed leader

Q. 209 *How do I make the transition from Financial Advisor to leader?*

This transition is not an easy one and should not be attempted without some leadership education or training. The role of a leader is dramatically different from that of the Financial Advisor. You will benefit greatly by reading two or three of the hundreds of books available on the topic of leadership. You should also interview at least one political and one organizational leader. Leaders exist in all walks life. Your own leadership style will emerge and develop over time. In the interim, you will learn a tremendous amount by reading about leaders, learning the various styles of leadership and speaking with actual leaders.

Q. 210 *As a leader, how should my behavior change toward team members?*

First, check your ego at the door. You will need to shift your mindset from that of Financial Advisor or administrator to one of team leader. Of course, the existing members of your team will be fully aware that you are transitioning into this leadership role. You must listen, process, plan, position and communicate...and then lead. As the leader you must attentively observe how the team operates and then provide feedback to the appropriate team members.

Q. 211 *Can a coach or coaching firm enhance my leadership skills?*

Maybe. That depends on the quality of the coaching and the willingness of the leader to accept direction. We believe that for the willing new leader, coaching is a valuable service. Make sure that the coach has experience in leadership development before you sign any contract.

Q. 212 *How does a coach or a coaching organization take me to the next level?*

Have a conversation with the leadership team of a coaching organization and participate in equal parts (talking and listening) before selecting someone to help you improve your performance.

It is important to recognize the distinction between coaching and training. Training comes in a box and is a one-size-fits-all program. There are many Financial Advisors who can benefit from pure training. Successful training can take an individual or a group to a specific plateau that is predetermined before the training is contracted. Specific skills to be developed during the course of the training should be outlined by the training provider before commencement of any program. Coaching, on the other hand, will be a more personal experience whereby the coach works one-on-one with you (or individuals within your group) to achieve an outcome that addresses you or your group's specific needs. Therefore a coach needs to possess deep analytical skills in order to determine two critical points along the spectrum of your team's culture:

- Your current situation
- Your desired outcome

Accurately determining these two points is no easy task. A skilled coach will take the time required and be able to communicate to you their understanding of your situation. The main ingredient that a successful coach should add to your journey toward Maximum Efficiency is a written plan. The written plan should guide you toward your Vision.

Q. 213 *What traits should I look for when hiring a coach?*

A coach should be:
- willing to take a passive role among the team (remain in the background)
- a positive role model who understands your position in the marketplace
- trustworthy

A coach should possess:
- effective analytical skills
- strong organizational skills
- planning skills
- a deep awareness of your industry
- expertise in developing talent

A coach should demonstrate:
- respect
- staying power
- an ability to learn your processes

Q. 214 *Why is it important that a coach have the ability to learn my processes?*

Every Financial Advisor processes workflow differently. There may be some areas in which a coach can immediately recommend an improved method for completing a task, but ideally that should happen only after the coach has a full understanding of how you currently process work.

Q. 215 *Why would a Financial Advisor revert to old habits when the coach leaves?*

This behavior usually occurs when the Financial Advisor did not accept the coach, or the Financial Advisor did not "buy-in" to the strength of the coach's processes and systems in the first place.

It does not take a lot of talent for a coach to come in and say, "Move over. I will show you how to do everything." In that case, when the coach walks out the door the Financial Advisor will normally revert to old habits.

Interview your coaching prospects carefully to determine their coaching style and be prepared to change to someone new if your current coach is not the right fit.

15

Your Responsibility to Your Clients

It is essential to understand what the plan sponsor organization values in relation to their 401(k)/Company Retirement Plan. Take notice of their corporate values and align with the culture of the organizations you are serving. Your products and solutions must fit their organizational culture as well as solve the plan sponsor's problems. Plan sponsors expect four qualities from you:

- Honesty
- Dependable service
- Efficiency
- To make them look good in the eyes of their employees

Begin by taking honesty to the point of full disclosure. Some Financial Advisors will lull a plan sponsor into a false sense of security by promising them that they will "do everything." This can be particularly perilous for the plan sponsor in an area where there is a substantial downside risk for non-compliance or ignorance. In existing relationships the plan sponsor should be equally concerned about what is being omitted from their plan as what is being provided. Above and beyond the normal contractual agreements, it makes sense to have a clear understanding of requirements and expectations among all involved parties.

Dependable service is what every plan sponsor assumes they are signing up for with any new vendor relationship. That assumption frequently proves to be inaccurate as evidenced by the 10 percent plus turnover in plan providers every year. (This is where the Service Agreement, outlined in Appendix A, will benefit you and the plan sponsor.)

Efficiency is important to the plan sponsor since many of the sponsoring companies are students and practitioners of Lean Services/Manufacturing, Six Sigma or Total Quality Management. For many of the plan sponsors you work with, their entire competitive-business-advantage is founded upon being the most efficient in their industry. They increase profit margins by incurring lower costs than their competition. Efficiency is more than a passing buzzword or flavor-of-the-month to the production or processing manager.

Finally, the plan sponsor wants their 401(k)/Company Retirement Plan to be perceived as a true benefit. By furnishing employees with a top-quality plan, management and the company will be well regarded by employees. Happy employees are productive employees.

Define your deliverables... Know what you do... And know it well! Support the functions that you deliver impeccably and never lose sight of the fact that your clients have options — which may not include you or your services.

Earlier in the Business Plan chapter (Chapter 4) you defined many components of your Business Plan. You also described the target market for your business (including the type of industry, size of employee base, average employee compensation, proximity to your office and/or home and other parameters). Now you will define, clarify and communicate how you will reach out to these prospects. When you have reached the point that these prospects become clients, it is vitally important to make clear to them how you will service them.

It is your responsibility to clearly communicate to the plan sponsor what your services are, and then deliver those services flawlessly to your clients. You will also be responsible for developing and delivering appropriate service strategies to each of your 401(k)/Company Retirement Plan clients. It is best to assume that all of this responsibility falls upon your shoulders. (In reality, it probably does not, but by assuming that it does, you should stay one step ahead of your competition.)

Q. 216 *What is my responsibility to the plan sponsor/client?*

The duties of the Financial Advisor will vary depending upon whether or not they are a fiduciary. If acting as fiduciary, the Financial Advisor is legally obligated to serve, first and foremost, the interests of the plan participants. Contractual responsibilities are very simple to define — read the contract! The ethical responsibility that you have to your client is a big one. The most successful Financial Advisors are those who have elevated their ethical responsibility to an attitude of Service Quality Pride℠ (SQP) with which they will serve their client. SQP is a higher level of responsibility to the client and entirely ethical. Good ethics carry the implication of "doing right by the customer." Having an SQP attitude toward your work and the customer translates into "doing right — for a different reason." That is — you and your team desire to be the best you can be for the benefit of the plan participants and the plan sponsor. In this type of environment, your attitude is a built-in customer guarantee.

Q. 217 *As the Financial Advisor, where should my loyalties lie among the employees, the plan sponsor and myself?*

The Financial Advisor has legal and practical loyalties to the participating employees, the plan sponsor and themselves. However, you must always remember that when you are considering an issue or making a decision, the interests of the plan participants come first.

Q. 218 *What are conflicts of interest and should I be concerned about them?*

Conflicts of interest are those situations which may benefit you but not your client. For example, if you are charged with assisting the plan sponsor in their selection of the best program provider, then your recommendation should be based upon your knowledge of the market, awareness of the program providers and the analysis you have conducted. Your recommendation cannot be based upon or influenced by which wholesaler treated you to the best steak dinner last month or paid your green-fees at the swankiest golf club. There are two extremely important issues to always consider: your client's interests and your reputation.

Q. 219 *What other conflicts of interest may arise?*

Compensation or revenue sharing arrangements, if not fully disclosed, can be an area of potential conflict of interest. Your safest avenue is to fully disclose all revenue sharing, fees and expenses associated with 401(k)/Company Retirement Plans. Also, be sure to speak with your compliance department to ensure that you fully comprehend your firm's requirements. You cannot serve anyone's interests properly if you are unemployed. After compliance be sure that your conscience is clear. If something does not feel appropriate or fair in your mind, then perhaps a conflict of interest exists. Keep in mind that when you are supplying services to plan sponsors or plan participants you are most likely a fiduciary. When serving as a fiduciary, whether named or deemed, you will be held to a higher standard of ethics. If your actions are always consistent with that of someone serving in a fiduciary role, you will be best positioned to serve the plan participants.

Q. 220 *What is my responsibility to the plan sponsor as it relates to plan investments?*

This depends on the documented capacity in which you are serving. We feel that you should always deliver the highest quality service to your client regardless of whether you are serving as a registered representative, an agent or an investment advisor. Although each of those capacities carry a different level of service standard, if you want to build a business of satisfied 401(k)/Company Retirement Plan clients, you should under-promise and over-deliver. We feel it is always best to deliver to a service standard that is higher than your contractual agreement. As always, confirm that your actions are in compliance with the internal requirements of your firm.

Q. 221 *How do I determine what the plan participants want?*

Your question here is twofold, because you are not only interested in what the plan sponsor wants the plan to accomplish for the plan participants, but also what the plan participants want for themselves. Ask your plan sponsor/client what they would like the plan to accomplish. Survey the plan participants to understand their needs as a group. If you meet with plan participants one-on-one, you will have the opportunity to become familiar with their specific needs and wants. Never lose sight of the fact that you have two clients in every 401(k)/ Company Retirement Plan.

Q. 222 *Will the plan sponsor see me after the sale?*

That is for you and your plan sponsor to decide. Some plan sponsors expect to see you once a year and others require more frequent contact. What commitments have you made with regard to ongoing service during the sales process? Most importantly at this stage, deliver what you promised. If you told your prospect that they would see you quarterly, then you have an obligation to see them at least once a quarter. The Service Agreement (see Appendix A) will specify the terms.

Q. 223 *What is the single most important point that I must know about a 401(k)/Company Retirement Plan product that I recommend?*

You must know why this product, the one that you are recommending, is the best fit for the client. You must have a clear understanding of that and you must know it cold! Depending on your internal compliance parameters, it may be wise for you to document the reason that this plan was selected and the steps that were taken to arrive at your conclusion

Q. 224 *Should I be a trailblazer or a follower-of-the-crowd when it comes to my client's plan investments?*

Neither of these extremes seems comfortable to most clients. Somewhere in-between the two is where most Financial Advisors and their clients have confidence and success. There is very little upside in being a trailblazer in the 401(k)/Company Retirement Plan business. However, if you have an expertise for recognizing the next top-performing manager or fund and would like to recommend them to your client, then you are best served by carefully documenting your selection process.

Q. 225 *Are my services priced fairly?*

We have been asked that question many times before, and our answer frequently begins by stating, "Price is an issue only in the absence of value." It is best to be priced "in-the-market," however you may choose, for reasons defined in your Business Plan, to be priced at either the extremely high or low end of the market.

Your profit margin should not be a starting point for determining the fairness of your pricing structure. Assess your pricing by utilizing the following three steps:

First you must understand your expenses and what you need to charge in order to cover your fully loaded costs. Second, you must determine a reasonable profit that you and your team deserve for providing such services. If, after including all costs and a reasonable profit, you are still well below market pricing, then you should consider raising your price to be on par with the overall market. Such a pricing structure puts you in a position to improve margins due to increased efficiencies.

Q. 226 *How can I be sure that I will meet the expectations of the 401(k)/Company Retirement Plan plan sponsor/client?*

We feel that the development of a written agreement (which we describe as a Service Agreement in Appendix A) will help you to establish client expectations and retain your 401(k)/Company Retirement Plan business. We feel strongly that there is great benefit in having a mutual understanding between the plan sponsor/client and the Financial Advisor's team. The Service Agreement should be straightforward, simple to comprehend and make crystal clear the responsibilities of each party to the agreement.

Q. 227 *How do I develop my Service Agreement?*

Developing your Service Agreement within the framework of your organization is no simple task. As you formulate your Service Agreement you need to be aware of the multiple customers within its structure. You must satisfy the requirements of the 401(k)/Company

Retirement Plan, and the needs of the plan participant, the plan sponsor/client, your organization, your own team and, indirectly, all regulators (collectively referred to as your "customers"). You should always be attentive to the needs of all of the customers with whom you interact.

The successful 401(k)/Company Retirement Plan program for any plan sponsor will assist the plan sponsor's company in achieving their own strategic objectives. Usually those objectives will include attracting, retaining and rewarding those productive employees who have a direct impact on the profitability of the sponsoring company. A good working relationship between the Financial Advisor and the plan sponsor/client will result in individual and shared responsibilities executed by you and the plan sponsor/client.

In order to deliver a highly effective 401(k)/Company Retirement Plan, the Financial Advisor's team and the plan sponsor/client should collectively establish all expectations and participate in regularly scheduled dialogue to continually confirm or revise those expectations. The Service Agreement will assist all parties involved in the delivery of the very best 401(k) plan possible to plan participants.

Once you have secured a new client, immediately demonstrate to them that you have a plan for servicing their needs. Inform the new client that you will meet with them (and all other appropriate personnel) to draft a service strategy document that will outline all requirements for serving their specific needs. Employers have differing needs, dependent upon overall size of the company, number of locations, number of non-English speaking employees, number of shifts and the education level of employees. Any specific issues that may arise will need to be taken into consideration when drafting the Service Agreement.

You will be more successful than your competition if you establish and maintain effective communication between you (your team) and the plan sponsor/client. The Service Agreement helps to reduce confusion concerning expectations. It constantly reinforces your value to the plan sponsor/client by keeping your deliverables in front of them. The Service Agreement helps you collectively establish common goals and defines the associated successful outcomes. It defines roles, responsibilities and puts the plan sponsor "on notice."

Once the Service Agreement has been drafted it will be up to you to properly manage your service strategies. The more substance that you can add to the Service Agreement, the more indispensable you will be to your plan sponsor/clients and their plan participants. (Please refer to Appendix A for sample Service Agreements.)

16

Your Responsibility to the Industry

Your responsibility to the industry can be summed up in a single word — Ethics. Your unwritten and usually unspoken responsibility is that you will respect the position of trust that plan sponsors and plan participants have placed you in. There is no greater honor that any company or individual can bestow upon you than to say, "I would like you to manage my money." It is an honor, not a privilege.

The first thing that comes to mind when considering the cases of Enron, Canary Capital, Refco, Barings and WorldCom is the betrayal of trust. In all cases it was personal greed or the acceptance of a collective greed that served as the catalyst for poor decision-making, which led to a grotesque financial outcome.

Ethics used to be all about doing what was right. Today a perceived absence of oversight by leaders and managers has generated a great degree of confusion and finger-pointing among the corporate executive team, middle managers, state Attorneys General and regulators.

You will be charged with managing many complex processes, intricate systems and numerous individuals over the course of your career (refer to the 401(k) Diagram in Appendix C). Your clients, as well as the industry, make a broad assumption that you fully comprehend every financial decision and investment product with which you are faced. As we all know, it would take more than a lifetime to do so.

The business ethics landscape of today is dramatically different than that faced by our industry just five years ago. Business ethics had traditionally been the domain of academicians and social critics. Frequently, philosophy was even brought into the discussion.

We all have compliance departments and regulatory agencies to keep us on the straight and narrow for our daily processing and activities. Every one of us also needs to stay in contact with that "inner voice" that may suspect a decision to be wrong, a process to be flawed or a behavior to be ethically questionable.

It is your responsibility to the industry to make sure that you, your team and your organization constantly protect the name and reputation of all involved.

Q. 228 *What is my responsibility to the industry?*

Financial scandals like Canary Capital, Arthur Andersen, late-trading and Enron have taken their toll and damaged the reputation of our industry. Your responsibility to our industry is to keep it free from fraud and deceit. In other words — keep it clean. Take the time and effort to hire good people with a conscience who fully respect the concept of ethics.

Devise and develop appropriate service strategies for your clients and fair compensation schedules for your team. If you do not currently have one, prepare a plan to inform your prospects of your capabilities and fees.

Q. 229 *What recent events or legislation speak to the topic of ethics?*

There are plenty of them, unfortunately! Enron, Refco, WorldCom, Sarbanes-Oxley.

Q. 230 *Has there been an impact on Financial Advisors from these recent ethics violations?*

Absolutely. Both the Sarbanes-Oxley related legislation and SEC review of pension consultants have occurred as the result of such violations.

Q. 231 *How can I assist a plan sponsor in learning of the past performance and credibility of a Financial Advisor or consultant?*

Direct them to www.nasd.org. and go to "Investor Information." The web site should provide the plan sponsor with all regulatory information that is currently available for a particular Financial Advisor. For registered investment advisors, the Form ADV, section II should provide sufficient information.

Section V –
Maximum
Efficiency^{SM}

17

Building
Your Business

The ability to prioritize the components of your business is crucial to your success. Your clients do not care how much revenue your business generates or how much money you make on your 401(k)/Company Retirement Plans if you are helping them to achieve their goals. This is a very important concept for you to learn, comprehend and implement in securing your income while ensuring your future success.

The Department of Labor, the Securities and Exchange Commission and the National Association of Securities Dealers do not care how much money you make on any of your accounts including 401(k)/Company Retirement Plans. Regulators have an interest in what you are *charging* – but not in what you are *making!* Your time and effort should be focused on how efficient you are and the margins you enjoy. Those Financial Advisors who will be surviving into the next five years, and thriving into the next 10 years will be those who continue to improve the efficiency levels of their business without negatively impacting service.

A question for many of us who service plan sponsors is, "What can/should I charge?" What is coming under continuing pressure in our industry is what we charge, not how much we make or keep. It is important for you to comprehend the difference. There is a shift occurring in our business today where plan sponsors see fees as being a hot topic. After "snoozing on the job" for the previous 25 years, the plan sponsors have awakened to the fees being charged in relation to their 401(k)/Company Retirement Plans. Currently there are an increasing number of plan sponsors who are concentrating on the overall effectiveness of the program versus attempting to purchase the least expensive offering in the market.

There is a question of cost versus benefit and a new understanding of the real value being delivered by the Financial Advisor. Recent research has supported the fact that plan sponsors are willing to pay higher fees in return for a service or program they can be proud of.

Q. 232   What is your process for generating new business?

Every growing organization or Financial Advisor needs a process for acquiring new clients (regardless of your industry, product or service). There are a variety of methods for setting your goals and achieving new business growth targets. If you have a tool that works for you, by all means, keep using it. We find a calendar approach to be helpful and have developed what we call the New Business Acquisition Calendar.

Q. 233   *What is the New Business Acquisition Calendar (NBAC)?*

The NBAC represents new business/client-related acquisition activity initiatives that you should be conducting day by day, week by week, month by month, quarter by quarter and year by year. These activities should ultimately help you to achieve your goals. If you like, your NBAC can integrate your personal activities with your professional activities (for a Total Activity Calendar.) The NBAC will help you to achieve your goals, and it displays your progress as you check off the daily activities that you accomplish.

Q. 234   *How do I build my NBAC?*

Purchase or print out an 18-month calendar. List the initiatives that you need to accomplish on each respective day of your calendar. The acquisition activity initiatives defined in your Business Plan are the basis of your NBAC. Every day that you accomplish your acquisition activities, check off the day on your calendar. The weekend, month-end and quarter-end should be documented by a complete set of check marks through your initiatives for the day, week, month and quarter. Your actual NBAC for contacting your prospects will be a function of many different components and assumptions.

(See Appendix B, Business Development by the Numbers, for a full explanation of building your business with the New Business Acquisition Calendar.)

Q. 235 *What questions do I need to ask when speaking with a 401(k)/Company Retirement Plan prospect?*

You probably have "favorite" questions that you like to ask the plan sponsor/prospect.

The following is a list of questions that we feel will provide you with quality information for determining your interest in moving forward in the 401(k)/Company Retirement Plan sales process.

Initial Introduction Questions

- Is the ABC Company 401(k)/Company Retirement Plan considered an employee benefit?
- Could you share with me the history of the ABC Company 401(k)/Company Retirement Plan?
- Why did ABC Company establish the 401(k)/Company Retirement Plan?
- What goals have you accomplished with it?
- Is your plan serving your need for employee retention?
- Is your plan serving your need to attract quality employees?
- Is your plan serving your need to reward employees?
- What firm is currently providing investment services for the ABC Company 401(k)/Company Retirement Plan?
- In what capacity is the investment team serving on your plan?
- Who (or what firm) is serving in a fiduciary capacity to your plan?
- What firm is currently providing administrative services for the ABC Company 401(k)/Company Retirement Plan?
- How often do you conduct due diligence for the plan?
- Who are the individuals that decide which organization(s) provide(s) services for the ABC Company 401(k)/Company Retirement Plan? (Who are the plan decision-makers?)

- How do you decide when it is time to upgrade your company's 401(k)/Company Retirement Plan?
- Will you be conducting a search for a new program provider this year? (If not, when will you?)
- How do your employees feel about the 401(k)/Company Retirement Plan?
- Are there any circumstances (current business relationships or family ties) that preclude you from objectively analyzing or moving your plan?

Plan Specific Demographic Questions

- How many employees are eligible for your plan?
- How many participants do you have in the plan?
- What is the eligibility requirement to join the ABC Company 401(k)/Company Retirement Plan?
- How many non-deferring eligible employees do you have?
- How many participants have an account balance?
- What is the average deferral percentage for non-highly compensated employees?
- How many locations do you have?
- What languages do your employees speak?

Plan Operations

- How often during the year can eligible employees enter the plan?
- Do you process payroll internally or through an outside vendor? (Which vendor?)
- How often do you transmit payroll contributions to your current 401(k)/Company Retirement Plan?
- What are the sources of contributions to the plan?
  - Employee Salary Deferral
  - Employer Discretionary
  - Employer Match
- (If applicable) Please describe the company match formula.
- Do participants direct the investment of all contributions to their accounts?

- How often can employees change their savings rate?
- How often can employees change how their money is invested?
- Do employees have access to account information via the phone?
- Do employees have access to account information via the Internet?
- How often do employees receive statements?
- How soon after a reporting period do employees receive their statements?
- Are the participant statements mailed directly to the participant's home or are they distributed by the employer?
- What do your employees say about the statements?
- Does the ABC Company 401(k)/Company Retirement Plan allow for participant loans?
- Does the plan allow for hardship withdrawals?
- Have any withdrawal provisions been abused?

Plan Investments

- Can I review your Statement of Investment Policy?
- What are the names/ticker symbols of the current investment options?
- With what frequency are the options reviewed?
- How are the options selected?
- How are the 401(k)/Company Retirement Plan assets currently allocated among the investment options ranging from conservative to aggressive?
- What is the most recent value of the plan assets?
- Do you have an Investment Advisor on your account?

Plan Service

- (If for a 401(k) plan) How have you notified employees that the plan is seeking Safe Harbor relief under the Department of Labor 404(c)?
- What type of issues arise, i.e. payroll transmission, compliance testing, etc., that you would change if you could?
- How accessible is the service contact for the plan?

- What expectations would you have for a new service provider?
- Who are the decision makers for "plan services"?
- Upon what basis would you make your decision for a new service provider?
- What enhancements do you want to make to the company 401(k)/Company Retirement Plan?
- By what date do you want the new plan program in place?
- Who will be involved at ABC company (and outside) in deciding who the next 401(k) vendor(s) will be for the 401(k)/Company Retirement Plan?
- What are the names of the organizations that have shown interest in being your next program provider?

Q. 236 **Are your introductory questions giving you the information you need?**

Do the responses that you are obtaining effectively tell you what you need to know? Some individuals have an evasive way of responding to inquiries. If that is the case, then you need to probe deeper, question someone else or have the responses sent to you in writing. Put another way, are you comfortable with way your plan sponsor contact is answering your questions? If you feel that you are obtaining accurate and direct answers, then you will have sufficient information for moving forward. If you feel that you are not obtaining quality responses, then take action to make sure that you do.

Q. 237 *Should I conduct an exit interview?*

Win or lose, conduct an exit interview. Never pass up an opportunity to get better. Once you have taken your product to the 401(k)/Company Retirement Plan plan sponsor and you have received a "yes" or "no" decision from them, you will still want to have one more process oriented question and answer session with them. Your intent is to find out what drove their decision. In either event (win or lose) the question and answer session during the exit interview is vitally important to you and the growth of your business. When probing for this high-quality information keep the following in mind:

- Be honest.
- Never be accusatory (even if you are not chosen).
- Use "open end" questions to stimulate high level conversation whenever possible.
- If you must use "closed end" questions, do so in relationship to a scale (i.e. "Ranked from 1 to 5, with 1 being Poor and 5 being Excellent, how would you rate our responsiveness to your questions?").
- Although it may be at the heart of your questioning, do not ask "Why didn't you hire me?" Focus instead on "Why did you hire *(name of the winning team)*?"

Remember, there are no right or wrong answers, but each answer will help refine your acquisition efforts.

Sample Questions

- What could we change with our product to make it more attractive?
- What could I have done better?
- What should we eliminate from our services?
- Where do our services lag behind the competition?
- How does our employee education compare to the competition?
- How do you feel our investments compare?
- How do you feel our fiduciary service compares to the competition?
- How does our Service Agreement compare to our competitors?
- Where do our services exceed our competitors?
- What was the one thing we did that made you want to hire us?

Remember, it is vitally important to conduct these interviews whether you win the 401(k)/Company Retirement Plan business or not.

18
Measurement

Monitoring facilitates accountability and defines how you will assess your progress in achieving your activities and goals. Specific tasks have been assigned to you and your team members. You have to be able to assess your progress in accomplishing your tasks. Stated another way, you must be accountable to your own goals. Primary Measurement Points (PMPs) are instrumental in tracking and monitoring your success.

Many of your plan sponsors will employ a form of the Balanced Scorecard to manage the various components of their business. Those components include measures in the areas of Financial, Processes, Systems, Human Resources, the Customer, the Competition, Communications and Strategy.

PMPs measure your progress. For managing your business they are the guardrail on the side of the road and the beacon that continually guides you to your success. PMPs must be defined for both your acquisition and retention activities. Over time, you will determine the appropriateness and applicability of your PMPs. With reasonable deliberation, you can determine if your PMPS are delivering the data required to manage your business. Are they paying off for your time and effort?

What should you do if you are not achieving your activity and production objectives? Take inventory of what you are measuring to fully understand what has negatively impacted your ability to achieve your goals. Assess the relationship between each measured activity and the achievement of your goals. Be determined to retain those PMPs that help you to successfully manage your business and continually refine or replace them where appropriate. Then get back to the task at hand, which is achieving your activity and production objectives while progressing to the accomplishment of your goals.

Q. 238 *Why should I measure anything?*

You need to establish thresholds for acceptable performance. Establishing these thresholds is the point of embarkation for measuring your performance. You need to determine a minimum acceptable performance standard and then make sure that all minimum requirements are being met. Only then can you attempt to move on to improving performance. The specific segments of your business that you measure will become your PMPs. The measurements that you take will then provide you with data that is convertible to useable information.

Q. 239 *Why do you make measurement sound so important?*

Because quite frankly, it is. The only way to know if you are improving in either production or process is by measuring the production or process. The primary method for impacting the production (end result) is by altering or improving the underlying processes. The only way to gauge improvement is by measurement. In the absence of measurement you may believe that everything is always going well when actually everything is not going well. If you have no methodology for comparing today's results with any other day, then how do you really know the status of your team's performance? If you were content with your production and team structure today, you probably would not be reading this book.

Q. 240 *What specific areas can I accurately measure?*

Although this list is not exhaustive, it does represent a good starting point for drilling down and setting measurements:

- Acquisition activities
- Business development
- Business Plan development
- Database development
- Enhancing cross-selling
- Knowledge acquisition
- Profiling
- Proposals
- Prospecting
- Retention activities
- Sales presentations
- Service to plan participants
- Service to plan sponsor

The accuracy of the measurement is completely up to you! But we do not think it makes sense to have traveled this far on your journey and then accept measures that are "close enough."

Consider the concept of a highway guardrail that is used to aid drivers along a dangerous curve or highway. Take note of the placement of the guardrail. It is located as an early warning system, just off the side of the road so that a driver who is unfortunate enough to use the services provided by a guardrail may have sufficient time to react and recover from their mistake. The guardrails are never placed at the bottom of a deep ravine to break the fall. Measurement in your business should be placed in similar locations.

Make sure your metrics assist you in managing your business. Do not position your measurements so that they report how bad things are after they have occurred. Your controller or finance person already provides that service.

Remember to begin with three to five measurements. Five is the optimal number. Once you and your group have become fully comfortable with the measures you have, you may want to add new ones. If you do, you may also want to eliminate old measures if they are not serving your business needs. Everyone and every team is motivated by their own set of unique metrics. You never want to have more than is productive. Three to five PMPs is ideal; eight is at the upper end of the scale.

Separate history from helpful business management measures. Again, make the measures meaningful contributors and good data collection points for assessing progress toward your goal. A quarterly measure of new business closed (in-the-door) is not a worthwhile measure. That measurement does not provide you with sufficient time to react to a bad quarter. A better indicator would be the number of written proposals delivered to prospects in a week. The quarterly measure of new business closed will provide you with a report of the financials after the quarter has closed out. It is essentially a historical document. Effective measures (such as the number of written proposals delivered to prospects in a week) will provide you with data and information related to performance before the quarter or month has been closed out, when there is still sufficient time to take corrective action and do something about it. Your measures should be early warning systems, not history books.

Q. 241 *What is a baseline and why is it so important if we want to improve?*

The baseline provides you with the first reference point that you will use along your journey to Maximum Efficiency. Keep in mind that the baseline is completely different from the benchmark. The baseline is "where you and your team are starting from." Theoretically, it is the lowest point of performance or efficiency. Without a baseline reference point, there would be no beginning point for your journey.

Q. 242 *What is a benchmark?*

Benchmarking is the measurement of your performance, compared to the industry. The biggest challenge with benchmarking is in obtaining accurate data from the industry. There are a variety of reasons for this (too numerous to mention) but a common reason is that Financial Advisors and their organizations do not readily share propriety data with individuals or entities outside of their group or organization.

A trusted source for such information would become your benchmark. We recommend that you begin to work from your baseline first and not be concerned with benchmarking right away.

Your organization (broker/dealer, bank, insurance company, TPA) should be in a position to assist you by providing benchmarks from within your own organization. That would be the best place for you to obtain such data in a quick and readily available format.

Execution

Tracking and Monitoring Your Activities using Primary Measurement Points (PMPs)

Q. 243 *What are Primary Measurement Points (PMPs)?*

Think of each PMP as a guardrail guiding your business to success. Your Strategic Plan is the roadmap that shows your route to your destination — the Vision. The PMPs will guide you on your journey toward success — on a day-to-day or week-to-week basis.

Q. 244 *In what areas of my business should I have PMPs?*

This is a fantastic question and gets to the heart of your business. It is interesting to see how different Financial Advisor teams view the primary drivers of their business. For a well-balanced Financial Advisor team we recommend considering measures in operations, financial, production, analysis and process. These major category headings should provide you with some direction as to what you need to measure within your own team. Unfortunately, every Financial Advisor and team is vastly different, and every team will have unique circumstances and challenges for improving overall performance. Where one team may have a great system for retaining good sponsor/clients but a poor process for generating new business, another team may struggle with retaining clients but generates new business from cold calling efforts very efficiently. This again points to the need for an accurate self-assessment (earlier in Chapter 1).

Q. 245 *How do I determine my PMPs?*

Determining your PMPs is not a simple task. They are well thought out metrics that will provide you with performance-related data throughout the operating segments of your business. When establishing your PMPs, you must possess a clear understanding and knowledge of what drives your business. You may develop PMPs for any segment of your business including cold calling, client retention, marketing, systems support, database management, rollover acquisition, investment management, etc.

After you have determined what tasks and activities will drive your success, then you must establish reasonable expectations around the metrics associated with the activities. These strategically placed metrics will become your PMPs.

Q. 246 *How many PMPs would you suggest for my 401(k)/Company Retirement Plan team?*

Always keep your PMPs limited to a manageable number. This means no more than five initially. If you determine during the measurement and improvement process that you would like to add metrics, consider adding two or three more. We happen to believe that five is the ideal number of PMPs for any organization. There are a limited number of metrics that can be monitored effectively, beyond which you can begin to negatively impact overall performance.

Q. 247 *Could you provide me with an example of what I might use as a Primary Measurement Point?*

PMP Example for Cold Calling — In this example it is most important for you to understand that the numbers are not as critical as is the information that you gather around the activity of establishing the cold call appointment. (So with the response to this question, please devote more time to digesting the concept than on computing the numbers.)

If you have a production goal ($48 million in new assets within the next 12 months) it would be simple to straight-line that goal. You would know that you needed to bring in $4 million per month for each of the next 12 months. However that type of monitoring and tracking system will only reveal results after they occur.

We are firm believers that your PMPs should serve as measures that will give you information before you have missed a goal. That way you will benefit by having sufficient time to modify your daily behavior so that you can stay on target for your original goal.

An example of a primary measurement point that can be linked to your overall goal of $48 million in new assets within the next

12 months, might be, "Establish five new prospect face-to-face appointments each week for plans with assets in excess of $5 million." This PMP (assuming a close ratio where such activity would generate closing 10 of these plans per year) will provide you with an early warning system if the required activity is not maintained week-to-week. This scenario assumes a cold call close ratio of less than four percent.

In this example, you know that if you are generating only five cold call appointments every two weeks, then you will need to close a higher percentage of your business or modify behavior within your team to generate the appropriate five cold call appointments per week. You are in a much better position to modify this behavior at the calling level versus modifying history once the numbers have become reality in the finance department.

Establishing PMPs takes much more time, effort and skill than setting your budget and straight-lining the financials.

Q. 248 *How do I determine the appropriateness and applicability of our PMPs?*

After establishing your PMPs, use them for a period of 30 to 60 days. Then assess their effectiveness. Does the data and information you are gathering help you manage your business? After 60 to 120 days of collecting data around the PMPs, you should be able to determine whether or not your PMPs are truly the correct measures for your business. It is normal for organizations and groups to tweak or adjust their PMPs in the early stages of implementation.

Q. 249 *What should I do if I am not achieving my activity and production objectives?*

Get introspective. Take the time to understand why you have not met your activity or production objectives. You need to determine what is getting in the way and unfavorably impacting your ability to perform. Assess the appropriateness of the activity and production measures toward the achievement of your goals. Make an informed decision whether or not to retain and/or alter those specific measures. Do not lose sight of the task at hand. Establishing the correct activity and production objectives will ultimately lead to accomplishing your goals.

Q. 250 *What Primary Measurement Points in my business determine whether I am succeeding or failing?*

Make an effort at this point to write down what you would like to measure. What would help you maintain a successful course for your business? Write down 5 key metrics that will enable you to manage the journey toward your Vision. These should work as a snapshot, where you can look at a chart or a trend-line and tell immediately if the function or process is operating as intended (or better or worse). If you get stuck on what to measure, refer to the prior question for the stimulation of ideas among the various segments of your business.

 WRITE IT

Q. 251 *Will these metrics provide me with sufficient time to modify behavior in order to avoid an unfavorable or disastrous outcome?*

If you do not have them properly structured, you will gain little useful information from the tabulated results. Remember, the metrics should serve you as an early warning system. You need to ask yourself, "What information will I have after I have collected this data for one week, three weeks, one month or three months? If you do not have a good snapshot of how you will modify behavior in the future as a result of the information that you have gathered, then revise your metrics.

19
Putting It
All Together

We have provided you with many of the components for successfully growing your 401(k)/Company Retirement Plan business. To use a jigsaw puzzle analogy — we have dumped out all of the pieces (including those all-important corners) on your coffee table. The next move is yours. You need to mentally envision your own end result (Vision) so that you can assemble the puzzle.

How you choose to proceed falls entirely on your shoulders. Continuing with the jigsaw puzzle analogy, do you search for all of the "blue sky" pieces or will you pick up pieces at random and attempt to figure out where and how they will be used? It is solely up to you to determine your next step. By now you have probably made extensive notes or marks in the margins, denoting areas you have targeted for improvement. Your next step is an executive decision on how to begin your continuous improvement project. Your major choices include:

- Attack your weakest link first (for instance, presentations, database, measurement, etc.), then progress to the next weakest component of your business. This is analogous to connecting all of the most difficult pieces initially (perhaps the blue sky) while ignoring the rest of the puzzle.
- Move chronologically through the Chapters of this book, which are structured in a logical, progressive order. This order can be very helpful if your interest is in a total business rework

solution. This would be analogous to first finding each of the four corners to the jigsaw puzzle – then moving inward.

- Moving to the area where you can achieve the greatest benefit the quickest. This approach requires a thorough understanding of your internal strengths and weaknesses. This is an excellent methodology for a strong leader or a strong manager. It is analogous to finding four or five puzzle pieces that connect and putting them together — regardless of their position in the puzzle. You know that you will achieve quick and substantial progress toward the end result.

Caution — whatever improvements you wish to achieve, assume that to implement them will require an additional 20 to 30 percent more time than originally estimated. Do not become discouraged when improvement does not come immediately. It takes time. You must tear down muscle before you begin to build it back stronger.

Your Maximum Efficiency Outline follows. It provides a quick summary for determining how to best achieve your goals.

The Maximum Efficiency outline is the template to use for implementing positive change within your business or your team. Because it is impossible to establish one single process that works for every business, we find that the Maximum Efficiency outline provides direction and reassurance to those Financial Advisors who are working toward continuous improvement.

Review the Maximum Efficiency outline to determine where you should begin. Do not be concerned with the order in which the topics appear or the various phases of the outline. Everyone will move along the continuous improvement spectrum at their own pace — dictated by and according to their own Vision and available time and resources.

If you encounter obstacles along the journey of improvement, please feel free to e-mail the authors to work through your issue.

- steffchalk@aol.com or
- empowering@knowhow.com

In most cases, well-placed and targeted questions put to you by an outsider can bring clarity to a fuzzy situation.

Maximum Efficiency^{SM} Outline

Phase 1—Strategic : Identify

- Assessment meeting
- Strategic plan review
- Confirmation of direction (Vision ➤ Mission ➤ Values)
- Resource inventory
- SWOT analysis
- GAP analysis
- Business focus / direction

Phase 2 — Planning : Document

- Team agreement
- Document GAP (from prior GAP Analysis)
- Major initiative worksheet
- Strategic Plan refinement
- Business Plan
- Determine Primary Measurement Points (PMPs)
- Match resources to initiatives
- Develop/finalize Strategic Plan

Phase 3 — Execute : Seize

- Next action worksheet
- Track Primary Measurement Points
- Close GAPs
- Maintain your view of the horizon
- Match resources to initiatives
- Pre-prospecting activities
- Pre-sales call activities

Phase 4 — Monitor : Maximize
(Ongoing Business Management)

- Measure
- Validate (check and re-check)
- Post-prospecting
- Post-sales call documentation
- Professional feedback
- Audit

Q. 252 *How will we know if our team is moving forward and "staying the course?"*

If:

- goals and objectives are defined in the Strategic Plan; and
- tasks and activities are defined in the Business Plan; and
- roles and responsibilities are communicated to team members; and
- leadership takes their position seriously...

then, the only missing ingredient is accountability!

You and the team must hold everyone accountable for his or her specific assigned tasks. Accountability is the backbone of your progress.

— Team Approach —

Q. 253 *How do I prepare the team?*

You will need to clearly communicate with your team that there is a new set of documented priorities that your group will be striving to achieve. Do not roll out your improvement process or strategy until you, as the leader, are fully prepared to take charge. It is better to postpone the rollout of the improvement process for 30, 90 or even 180 days if you are not yet ready to manage, oversee and lead the team. Everyone involved will be much more comfortable executing a well-defined, clearly communicated plan as opposed to a quick, haphazard effort that dies the death of "yet another one of those programs" that comes and goes. Your journey toward Maximum Efficiency needs to be separated from any previous improvement efforts that have failed in the past.

Q. 254 *How do I make the team part of the solution process?*

You know your team better than anyone. Even now you probably have a good understanding of who is leadership material and who will be more productive by being in a supportive role. (Every once in awhile you may be surprised to see a team member shift between leading and being led — but this does not occur frequently.)

Q. 255 *What is the most important aspect of attempting to attain Maximum Efficiency?*

The single most important element on your journey to Maximum Efficiency is clear, continuous and effective communication. Without solid communication your effort will not be heard, understood or accepted and the results will most likely be disastrous and counter-productive.

Take the time and effort to become an effective leader. Your team, the plan sponsor, the plan participants, the program providers and the industry is counting on you!

Appendix

Appendix A

401(k)/Company Retirement Plan Service Agreement

The 401(k)/Company Retirement Plan Service Agreement provides multiple benefits for the program provider and plan sponsor.

Your 401(k)/Company Retirement Plan Service Agreement is an effective tool for confirming requirements, and managing the time you spend retaining and growing your client relationships. When properly positioned, it is also a great marketing tool that you can furnish to plan sponsor prospects to demonstrate how you intend to serve them over a long period of time. If you use a printed Service Agreement you will distinguish yourself and your team from the majority of your competition — many of whom pursue 401(k)/Company Retirement Plan/Company Retirement Plan business on only a part-time basis.

The 401(k)/Company Retirement Plan/Company Retirement Plan Service Agreement should:

- Establish and maintain effective communication between you, your team and the plan sponsor.
- Reduce the ambiguity of duties and possible "confusion of expectations" by all partners.
- Remind the client of the value that you bring to the relationship.
- Define your deliverables.
- Establish responsibilities for you and your plan sponsors.
- Establish a working document for you and/or your team to follow.

When you can support your client functions with visual representations, the receiver of your message, either prospect or client, is better able to comprehend the precise ideas that you are communicating. The majority of what adults learn is through visual representation. Financial Advisors are all capable of "talking a mean game," but a characteristic that differentiates the upper echelon of 401(k)/ Company Retirement Plan Financial Advisors from all others is the ability to effectively communicate how they will serve their plan sponsor and plan participant clients.

Your plan sponsor clients have an obligation to prudently select and monitor all service providers to their company 401(k)/Company Retirement Plan. By establishing a written Service Agreement you can provide clients and prospects with documented due diligence attesting to their great decision to employ you to serve their company plan.

Having a Service Agreement in place which has been agreed upon by your plan sponsor clients will help you to optimize your time and return on your investment. Everyone involved in the relationship will appreciate knowing what you are doing for your clients.

As your business grows so will your need to effectively manage your time. Since time is a limited resource, you must prudently manage the amount you devote to any one plan sponsor.

Your 401(k)/Company Retirement Plan Service Agreement promotes your great value to your clients and partners and assists you with achieving your personal and professional goals.

Possible components of your 401(k)/Company Retirement Plan Service Agreement include:

- A "Statement of Rights"— a brief listing of what your plan sponsor and plan participant clients can expect to receive from you or your team. This component of your Service Agreement is very dependent upon what you want to deliver to your clients and what you want to be known for (some might call it your Value Proposition).
- A listing of specific service initiatives spanning the two-phased life-cycle of the 401(k)/Company Retirement Plan. (Phase 1 = Conversion or Start-up; Phase 2 = Maintenance)
- Statement of plan sponsor obligations that make the plan sponsor aware that they have obligations to the plan in order to maintain a great 401(k)/Company Retirement Plan.

Imagine that you are meeting a sponsor prospect for the first time. You say, "I would like to share with you our team's beliefs along with our capability to serve your company 401(k)/Company Retirement Plan through what we refer to as our 'Statement of Rights.'"

Then you list those primary service themes that will guide your activities with your plan sponsor clients:

- You have the right to expect us to assist you with the honest and effective management of your fiduciary responsibilities with respect to your company 401(k)/Company Retirement Plan.
- You have the right to expect us to raise the awareness of your employees about the 401(k)/Company Retirement Plan that you are offering to them.
- You have the right to expect a call back within 24 hours to any service issue or question you may pose.

Then include service themes that will guide your activities with plan participant clients:

- Your plan participants have the right to expect us to provide to them comprehensive and understandable guidance in accomplishing their retirement saving goals.
- Plan participants have the right to expect us to provide them access to the full range of resources available to best support them.

Your 401(k)/Company Retirement Plan service initiatives span the life cycle of the relationship you have with your plans. Your can divide your service initiatives into these categories:

- High-level
- Discovery
- Analyze
- Execution
- Management

High-level

High-level service initiatives are "the big picture" or "the 30,000 foot perspective" service tactics.

For example:

- We will objectively assist you with the selection and monitoring of appropriate solutions for the design, administration, investments, employee education and recordkeeping aspects of your 401(k)/Company Retirement Plan.
- We will monitor program providers, plan investments and employee retirement education.
- We will continually remind your employees of their opportunity to use their 401(k)/Company Retirement Plan for achieving their retirement saving goals.

Discovery

Discovery initiatives are those service tactics that you deliver at the beginning of the relationship with your 401(k)/Company Retirement Plan sponsors. As an example, you might state:

- When we are awarded the opportunity to serve a 401(k)/Company Retirement Plan, we wish to interview any employee currently responsible for communicating the plan with your employees. We need to discover current practices and then share "best practices" with your employees, such as:
    - Modes of communication — group versus individual meetings, company intranet, and hard-copy materials.
    - Timing of communication — the best day of the week and time of day for communicating with employees.
    - Leadership — if there are employees whose opinion is thought of highly by others, we would like to speak with them. We would like to share current 401(k)/Company Retirement Plan information with them so that they are in a position to disseminate accurate information.

(When developing events for employees, the following people should be involved: you, representatives from the program provider and anyone at the company who normally schedules, plans, and conducts employee meetings.)

- We will request a copy of your current plan document for review by our technical team to insure that it is in compliance with current tax laws.
- We will consult with your Investment Committee to comprehend the current decision making process concerning the plan investments. We want to meet with and act as a consultant to your Investment Committee on an ongoing basis.

(If the plan sponsor does not have an Investment Committee, then this is an opportunity for you to assist with the creation of one.)

Sample Discovery Initiatives
- Plan sponsor activities: welcome call
- Investment Committee meeting
- Investment Policy Statement review
- Determine investment mapping
- Meet with company representatives to develop survey
- Survey employees
- Develop employee education strategy

Analyze
The analysis initiatives assist you in understanding what strategy and tactics to recommend for achieving the results that you and the employer desire for the plan participants. For example, you might use surveys to acquire employees' current perspectives, and state to the employer that, "The survey results will provide a 'baseline' for measurement so that when we re-survey employees in the future we will be able to judge the effectiveness of our efforts."

Analysis initiatives provide the data and information necessary for you to confidently recommend strategy. The results of the analysis will provide you with "What" you want to accomplish as well as the "How" you will achieve that goal.

Execution
It is now time to execute your employee education tactics. Perhaps you have prepared a "Letter from the company president" to be distributed to employees announcing the new 401(k)/Company Retirement Plan program. You may choose to utilize retirement plan posters or payroll stuffers. You must schedule and deliver group meetings. When you are

onsite, you may want to set aside a series of 20-minute time slots to conduct one-on-one counseling sessions with plan participants. During these one-on-one meetings, you can speak directly to the participants about personal matters concerning their retirement savings and also address any other financial questions they may have.

Consider developing your employee education curriculum around a specific theme, such as these:

Save a %, Not a $ Amount

Plan participants should focus on saving a percentage of their earnings instead of being concerned with a specific dollar amount. Such a strategy can be more comfortable for a participant because by saving a percentage of earnings, the plan participant's savings will increase or decrease depending on how much they earn. Those participants that specify a hard dollar amount tend to find that as their incomes rise, the percentage they save for retirement declines. Saving a percentage of what they earn allows a plan participant's contribution to keep pace with their increased earnings.

A primary goal for plan participants should be to enable them to maintain their same spending habits in retirement. Maintaining pace with a rising cost of living is important.

Minimum to Save = Maximum from the Employer

The bare minimum that each employee should contribute to a plan is the amount that qualifies the participant for the maximum employer matching contribution. Employer matched contributions are virtually "free money" for a participating employee. If there is a company match in a 401(k)/Company Retirement Plan, participants automatically achieve greater savings and reach their retirement goals faster.

Low Cost

One of the most beneficial aspects of a 401(k)/Company Retirement Plan is the low-to-no cost aspect to plan participants. A 401(k)/Company Retirement Plan is usually one of the most efficient and least expensive tools plan participants can use to build their retirement nest egg. Compared to IRAs or savings accounts, 401(k)/Company Retirement Plan benefits far outweigh any costs paid by the individual plan participants.

Automatic Savings

Automatic saving that occurs through payroll deduction is a valuable benefit of a 401(k)/Company Retirement Plan. The plan converts employees from spenders to prudent savers by encouraging them to make saving their first priority. Many employees need this automated saving through payroll deduction.

Management

Management initiatives allow you to strengthen the relationship you have with the plan sponsor and secure your long-term position with their 401(k)/Company Retirement Plan. Your management initiatives will position you to become an indispensable asset to the plan sponsor. They should feel that they could not have as good a 401(k)/Company Retirement Plan without you.

Your program provider partner needs to supply to you plan level reporting which describes participation statistics including:

- number of eligible employees
- number of deferring participants
- deferral percentages by group for non-highly compensated employees
- deferral percentages by group for highly compensated employees
- demographic breakdown based on age
- demographic breakdown based on income

You should also obtain from the program provider information on how the "800" number and internet are being used by plan participants. This information can assist with the refinement of your education initiatives.

Additional management initiatives could include:

- Review the investments versus the Investment Policy Statement (IPS) with the Investment Committee.
- Survey employees to verify the perceptions uncovered during casual conversation at participant meetings. Always be prepared to establish improvement targets for the upcoming year.
- Have the employer report to you any company issues which could impact the 401(k)/Company Retirement Plan.

You, in turn, should always communicate marketplace issues that could impact the company and its associated plan.

Obligations of the Employer/Plan Sponsor

Not every prospect deserves to be one of your valued clients. Your challenge during prospecting and profiling is to aggressively narrow the number of prospects to those quality individuals whose business you want. Another aspect to assess during your investigation of a prospect is whether the employer plan sponsor respects the great value that you will bring to their 401(k)/Company Retirement Plan.

Here are some thoughts that you may want to communicate to prospect plan sponsors to inform them of the environment they need to provide if they become your client:

Employer plan sponsors should:
- Share with you their view of corporate goals for their 401(k)/Company Retirement Plan.
- Explain the history of their current 401(k)/Company Retirement Plan (if any), including their original beliefs and the evolution of those beliefs for their 401(k)/Company Retirement Plan.
- State their needs and the needs of their employees with regard to the 401(k)/Company Retirement Plan.
- Share in the development of goals for the 401(k)/Company Retirement Plan including an expectation of how accomplishing those goals will favorably impact their employees.
- Promote communication between you and any "outside" professionals who are involved with their company 401(k)/Company Retirement Plan, i.e. ERISA counsel, Third Party Administrators and CPAs.
- Support the accomplishment of employee education initiatives by providing you with access to appropriate company personnel.
- Promote employee meetings and foster a continuing effort of promoting the 401(k)/Company Retirement Plan.
- Notify you immediately of any event which results in a material change to the company and or employees. This is especially

important if such an event would impact your ability to execute your responsibilities.
- Provide to you ongoing feedback that will assist you in improving your service to the plan participants.

What follows is a sample Statement of Rights and two samples of 401(k)/Company Retirement Plan Service Agreements.

The 401(k)/Company Retirement Plan Statement of Rights

Our Beliefs

We believe that an effective 401(k)/Company Retirement Plan for the ABC Company will assist all in achieving strategic objectives by attracting, retaining, rewarding and motivating productive employees who have a direct impact upon the profitability of the company.

We believe that an effective 401(k)/Company Retirement Plan is the outcome of individual and shared responsibilities executed by you, the 401(k)/Company Retirement Plan program provider and our team.

We believe that you deserve the best service that our team can provide to assist in managing the 401(k)/Company Retirement Plan.

We believe that we should assist you in promoting use of the 401(k)/Company Retirement Plan among the eligible employees.

This Statement of Rights is offered as an expression of our commitment to you and your employees.

Your Rights

You have the right to expect that the company 401(k)/Company Retirement Plan will enhance the probability of the company's profitability by attracting, retaining, rewarding and motivating productive employees.

You have the right to expect that our team will assist you in the efficient and effective management of your fiduciary responsibilities with respect to ERISA .

You have the right to expect that we will present to you the most competitive 401(k)/Company Retirement Plan program solutions available.

You have the right to expect that our team will make your employees more aware of the 401(k)/Company Retirement Plan benefit program made available by you.

You have the right to expect that our team will increase the participation rate among the non-highly compensated employees.

You have the right to expect that our team will increase the average deferral percentage for the non-highly compensated employees.

You have the right to expect a response to your inquiries within 24 hours.

You have the right to receive a bi-annual analysis of your 401(k)/Company Retirement Plan program to insure that your company and the plan participants are benefiting from competitive marketplace dynamics.

— Service Agreement Sample #1 —

The 401(k)/Company Retirement Plan/Company Retirement Plan Service Agreement
between
The ABC Company Retirement Plan
and
(Your name or name of your team)

(Your or your team's name) provides honest and forthright counsel in developing and delivering comprehensive solutions to *(name of company)* employers and their employees. Our emphasis is on assisting each plan participant to achieve their respective goals through their corporate retirement plan.

Plan Sponsor: We will assist plan sponsor clients to achieve their goal of enhancing their company's profitability through their company retirement plan. We will achieve this goal by assisting plan sponsor clients to efficiently and effectively manage their fiduciary responsibility with respect to ERISA, and to make participants more aware of the benefit they are receiving from their employer.

Plan Participants: We will assist plan participant clients to confidently build and manage their retirement wealth. We will achieve this goal by helping plan participants to understand how their company retirement plan works to help them reach their retirement savings goal. We will also teach them how to effectively allocate their assets for retirement.

Our Team Responsibilities to Our Employer Clients

High-level

- Objectively assist with the selection of suitable 401(k)/Company Retirement Plan program providers
- Harness our local and national resources to coordinate all conversion, implementation and operational events
- Build upon the confidence that your employees have in their ability to accumulate and manage their retirement wealth, reflected in the following outcomes:
  - Raise the participation rate among all employees
  - Raise the savings rate among all employees and specifically among the non-highly compensated employees
  - Promote the achievement of an appropriate asset allocation model for the plan in general and each of the participants individually
- Ongoing assistance with the management of your prudent fiduciary processes
- Continually elevate employee awareness, and promote utilization of the 401(k)/Company Retirement Plan benefit program to achieve their personal goals
- Maintain strict confidentiality in all matters

Discovery

- Interview appropriate leadership and management team to comprehend corporate goals and objectives.
- Interview all appropriate representatives (management and participants) to understand employee retirement plan communication issues, hurdles and best practices, including:
  - Most effective employee communication
  - Day of week and time of day for group meetings
  - Identifying influential employees

Analyze

- Survey employees to discover and understand plan participant opinions and to determine first year employee education initiatives and set expected outcomes for:
  - Participation rates
  - Deferral percentage of non-highly compensated employees
  - Asset allocation based on plan demographics
- Development of an Investment Policy Statement (IPS) which includes guidelines for selecting and removing funds
- Assist in the selection of plan investments
- Supply appropriate investment reports for posting and viewing by the plan participants. Include the chosen investment choice with the associated comparative benchmark.

Execute

- Define with you an employee communication strategy to announce their "new" retirement program
  - "Letter from the President"
  - Payroll stuffers
  - Company intranet
  - Company newsletter
  - Posters
  - Retirement Plan highlights
- Prepare employee education curriculum initiatives
- Develop a timeline of employee communication and education initiatives
- Deploy an effective employee communication strategy
- Deliver a successful employee education program

Management

- Designate a specific team member to "triage" all inquiries
- Employ a 24-hour return call policy
- Report to plan sponsor on regulatory and industry "impact" issues
- Periodic Service Calls
- Periodic review of each fund in the investment menu versus the appropriate benchmark

- Annual survey of all employees to assess the effectiveness of education initiatives as well as to develop future initiatives
- Annual trustee meeting to review:
  - Investment Policy Statement
  - Fiduciary Worksheet
  - Employee Education Initiatives — Expectations vs. Outcomes
    - ÷ Participation
    - ÷ NHCE Salary Deferral percent
- Support the building and maintenance of the Plan Sponsor Book, to include:
  - Plan Document – with amendments
  - Trust Documents
  - Summary Plan Description, including all amendments, addenda and attachments
  - Adoption Agreement
  - Statement of intended compliance with DOL Regulation 404(c)
  - Plan Demographic Report
  - Survey Report(s)
  - Investment Policy Statement
  - Employee Education Initiatives
    - ÷ Presentations
    - ÷ Materials handed out
    - ÷ Employee sign-in sheets
  - Copy of ERISA Bond
- Documentation of 401(k)/Company Retirement Plan Program Provider selection
- Bi-annual preparation of the DOL 401(k)/Company Retirement Plan Fee Disclosure Form

Obligations of Employer

- Facilitate in the discovery of:
  - the intended corporate goals for the plan to achieve
  - the history of the company retirement plan
  - the needs of your company and employees

- Share in the development of specific plan sponsor and participant goals
- Facilitate communications with all involved parties
- Promote employee education initiatives
  - Provide access to personnel
  - Establish meetings during company time
  - Permit one-on-one meetings during company time
- Notify our Financial Advisor team in the event of any material change which could impact our ability to fulfill our responsibilities to you and your employees
- Provide ongoing feedback in order for our team to fine tune and improve our overall service

_____

ABC plan sponsor

_____

Your name or the name of your team

Date ____/____/____

— Service Agreement Sample #2 —

The 401(k)/Company Retirement Plan Service Agreement
By and between
ABC Plan Sponsor and XYZ Financial Services Team

XYZ (Team) Statement of Service

The XYZ Financial Services Team provides honest and forthright counsel in developing and delivering comprehensive solutions to ABC plan sponsor and their employees, assisting each to achieve their respective goals through their corporate retirement plan.

Plan sponsor: We will assist ABC plan sponsor to achieve their goal of enhancing their company's profitability through their company retirement plan. We will achieve this goal by assisting our plan sponsor clients to efficiently manage their fiduciary responsibility with respect to ERISA, and to make participants more aware of the benefit they are receiving from their employer.

Plan participants: We will assist ABC plan sponsor's plan participants in confidently accumulating and managing their 401(k)/ Company Retirement Plan assets. We will achieve this goal by helping plan participants to understand the benefits of their company retirement plan and how it operates. The XYZ Financial Services Team is committed to helping plan participants to achieve their retirement savings goal and we will teach them how to effectively allocate their assets for retirement.

The XYZ Financial Services Team agrees to the following:

One-time
• Establish a Statement of Investment Policy

Annually
• Meet with the Retirement Plan Committee, within 90 days of the calendar year-end. This meeting will be for the purpose of:
  ▪ Reviewing the Statement of Investment Policy
  ▪ Reviewing the results of the IRS compliance testing
  ▪ Reviewing investments
  ▪ Establishing the participant education curriculum for the next 12 months

Quarterly
• Meet with the Retirement Plan Committee, within 45 days of the calendar quarter-end. This meeting will be for the purpose of:
  ▪ Monitoring the plan investment performance
  ▪ Scheduling participant education for the following quarter
  ▪ Confirming the education curriculum for the next quarter

Daily
• Return plan sponsor telephone calls within 24 hours
• Return plan participant telephone calls within 48 hours

ABC Plan Sponsor Agrees to:

Annually

• Be available for the Annual Review within 90 days from the calendar year-end

Quarterly

• Be available for the Quarterly Review within 45 days from the calendar quarter-end

_____

ABC Plan Sponsor

_____

XYZ Financial Services Team

Date _____/_____/_____

Appendix B
Business Development By the Numbers

This section focuses on the quantitative aspects of growing your business.

— Goals —

Business development activities all begin as an outgrowth of your goals. You define your goals. Make them meaningful and specific. You must feel that you "own" your goals. They are both public to the group and personal to you. You determine what steps to take to achieve them. You must initiate and execute steps to accomplish them. A critical part of goal-setting is your understanding that you, personally, will do everything possible to meet, if not exceed, your goals.

Ensure that your goals are meaningful and specific by answering these questions:
- What is my goal? (be specific)
- Why is it my goal? (be honest)
- How will achieving the goal affect my team?
- What specific outcomes will occur as a result of achieving this goal?
- When will I accomplish the goal? (use a definite timeline)
- How will I accomplish the goal? (define your plan)
- What specific initiatives must I accomplish in order to meet my goal? (list the incremental steps involved)
- What actions will I perform during the specific initiatives?
- Am I willing to do what is necessary to accomplish my goal? (be honest)
- What is my reward for accomplishing my goal?

Once your goals have been defined, frame them with some easy to understand, straightforward language. Make them real. Make them simple to understand and comprehend. These become your goal statements. Goal statements include your goal and what achieving the goal will do for your team, business and personal life. Here are some examples of goal statements that "need work" and their revisions:

Net Compensation Goal Statement

One that needs work: I will add more 401(k)/Company Retirement Plans to my business mix this year.

One that is better: I will generate $60,400 in net compensation from my 401(k)/Company Retirement Plan business this year as a result of adding eight 401(k) plans and two Defined Benefit plans, each with $2 million in assets and 50 plan participants. These new plans will generate $160,000 in gross revenue, 10% of my total annual production goal of $1.6 million. I will generate ancillary business with 10% of the new 500 plan participants, for a total of $80,000 in gross revenue. The $210,000 ($160,000 + $80,000) of gross revenue generated from the 401(k)/Company Retirement Plan related business will equal $60,400 in net compensation after broker dealer payout and taxes are deducted. I will deposit $20,000 in my sons' 529-education account, $30,000 in the Vacation Home savings account and I will take my spouse to Hawaii for two weeks with the remaining $10,400.

After developing your goals and writing your goal statements, determine what level of production and commission revenue is needed to accomplish them. Your end result is to accurately define the Total Net Compensation you need to achieve in order to reach your goals. The Net Compensation Goal can then be used to determine what volume of 401(k)/Company Retirement Plan assets you need to bring in, assessed against your commission payout or fees. Once you have determined the volume of 401(k)/Company Retirement Plan assets to bring in, you can determine your gross compensation before taxes goal, your gross commission before payout goal, and your gross asset acquisition goal.

401(k)/Company Retirement Plan Revenue and Cross-Selling Revenue

Do you believe you can make more money simply from the cash flow of the 401(k)/Company Retirement Plan or make more from cross-selling opportunities? That didn't take long. You know you can make a lot more money from the cross-selling opportunities the 401(k)/

Company Retirement Plan plans afford you. And you have to build that opportunity into your revenue projections. If you do not, you will most likely leave a substantial amount of potential revenue "on the table." Once you have goals defined you can begin to establish the required activities for accomplishing them.

A great benefit in using your 401(k)/Company Retirement Plan New Business Acquisition Calendar (NBAC as referenced in Chapter 16) is that you will understand the interaction of your numbers. This will result in your either continuing or altering your strategy.

Example
Assumptions:
$250,000 in net new cumulative compensation from 401(k)/ Company Retirement Plan business over the next five year period.

Summary Components:

Net new cumulative compensation from cross-selling activities:	$100,000
Average Commission payout rate 401(k)/Company Retirement Plan:	.0075/.75%
Average Commission payout individual client:	.0085/.85%
Broker / Dealer payout:	40%
Marginal tax bracket:	40%
Average size employer-sponsored plan:	$5,000,000
Average number of plan participants:	100

Total 401(k)/Company Retirement Plan assets to accumulate over next five years: $80,000,000.00

Average size individual account acquired as a result of cross-selling activities:	$100,000
Average conversion rate/penetration rate of plan participants into individual clients:	10%

— Activities—

Activities are the actions taken and tasks completed that take you along the journey toward accomplishing your goals. In order to accomplish your goals, you must define your activities. The better you can define your activities, the greater the probability of maintaining your focus and achieving your goals. What do you need to do to achieve your gross asset acquisition goal? What do you need to do to achieve your cross-selling revenue goal? Defining your activities for both acquisition and retention is a critical step in your Business Plan.

Primary Measurement Points (PMPs), as outlined in Chapter 18, are projected, realistic outcomes that guide you along your journey to accomplishing your overall goals. For example, Acquisition PMPs may include conducting a minimum number of initial contacts, discovery meetings, preparing proposals and delivering sales presentations. Retention PMPs could include, conducting an annual Trustee meeting with the employer, quarterly investment review with the Investment Committee and semi-annual enrollment meetings with newly eligible employees, to name a few.

Now let's put this to a practical application. For example, say your goal is to generate $80 million of 401(k)/Company Retirement Plan assets into your book of business over a five-year span (in an effort to achieve your Net Compensation Goal.) Let's further assume that your average 401(k)/Company Retirement Plan is going to be $4 million dollars, which includes a range of $1 million to $8 million dollar prospect plans.

Regardless of what part of the country you are working in, there are 240 total net working days in a year; that is, 20 days a month times 12 months. And if you give yourself five years to achieve your goals, you have a total of 1200 net working days.

20 Working days per month x 12 months =
240 Working days per year x 5 years =
1,200 total working days in 5 years

If your goal is to acquire 20 new plans over the next 5 years, and you apply the 10% closure rule (from "cold" to client), you will need to begin with 200 cold prospects that satisfy all of your target and financial requirements. (This is using your five-year goal of acquiring 20 401(k)/Company Retirement Plans.)

If you have existing institutional business or a client base and strong social contacts (where you know a good number of decision-makers at companies which have 401(k)/Company Retirement Plans that fit your target criteria,) you may be working with a larger number of "warm" prospects. If this is your situation, you may need far fewer cold leads to achieve your goals than the Financial Advisor who is building a business without the benefit of an existing client or social base.

As your experience grows, you will develop your own more accurate Acquisition Activity Measurement screens. For our purposes we will assume the following, all based on the theme that not every prospect deserves to be your client. Assume conservatively that, of your cold prospects, only 40% will actually warm up and hold a Discovery Meeting with you. After the Discovery Meeting with your prospects, you will publish a proposal for, and conduct a subsequent sales presentation with, only 50% of them. One should be able to actually close a deal with about 50% of those plan sponsors to whom you have presented.

Activity Percentages
200 cold prospects
40% converted to warm prospects via discovery meeting = 80
50% converted to proposal or subsequent sales presentation = 40
50% converted to clients = 20 out of your original 200 cold prospects!

So we should take a look at a sample set of Acquisition PMP projections for Initial Contacts, Discovery Meetings, Proposals and Sales Presentations. (Feel free to adjust percentages according to your personal experience.)

As a result of a monthly drip mail and follow-up call marketing initiative, you determine that you will contact a decision-maker at one of your 200 cold prospect companies every six business-days. We derive that six business-day figure by dividing 1200 total working days by 200 cold prospects. The result of that division is six business days.

Of those 200 cold prospects, you will "warm" up 40%. Forty percent of 200 equates to 80 warm prospects. To determine how often you will meet with a warm prospect, take the 1200 total business days and divide that by the 80 warm prospects for a sum of 15. That means you will have on average a discovery meeting with one of your 80 warm prospects every 15 business days.

Of the 80 warm prospects you meet with, 50% will become "hot" prospects. You will then prepare a proposal and conduct a follow-up sales presentation for 40 hot prospects. We determine how often you will publish a proposal and conduct a follow-up sales presentation by taking our 1200 total working days and dividing that by our 40 hot prospects for a total of one proposal and a follow-up sales presentation on average every 30 business days.

If we assume that you will close deals with 50% of your hot prospects, that equates to 50% of 40 clients, or 20 closed 401(k)/ Company Retirement Plans. Again, we take the 1200 total working-days, divide that by number of clients, in this case 20, then we result in one new plan closed every 60 business days. That's one plan every three months, or four per year for five years.

When PMPs are in place they can be used to assess the progress of either acquisition or retention activities. PMP results (data) provide the information you need to ask the tough questions about how you manage your activities:

- Am I doing what is needed?
- Am I publishing a proposal and conducting a follow-up sales presentation every thirty business-days?
- Am I doing what is needed to open up individual accounts with 10% of plan participants?

If the answer to any question contains the word "no," another question is prompted: "Why not?"

Your activity PMPs instill a number of continuous self-reinforcing activity targets to keep you on plan. If you are achieving or exceeding your activity PMPs at one level, the subsequent activity PMPs should fall into place. Make necessary adjustments to your activities and activity PMPs to insure your achievement.

With PMPs in place, you have defined what makes for a great week, month, quarter and year concerning your acquisition activities. As an example based on what was just stated, you define a great week as mailing out to your designated cold prospects and placing follow-up calls to those your mailed the previous week. A great month is cycling through your entire database of cold leads and having initial contact with four of your cold prospect plan decision makers each month.

We encourage you to define a great year based on the previous breakdown and your personal experience!

Appendix C
401(k) Relationship Schematic

The 401(k) relationship is one of the most cumbersome structures in business today. One of the reasons is because there is not a single purchaser of services, nor is there a single provider of services. Many of the "arrangements" are established in a package structure with little control or input from the purchaser. The compensation which passes hands in these relationships has been poorly disclosed in the past. There are many industry groups that are attempting to improve the disclosure of compensation, but as an industry, today we are not there.

The following schematic is not perfect, nor is it accurate in 100 percent of 401(k) relationships. But it does accurately portray each of the components and sub-systems associated with a 401(k) plan — the most complicated employee benefit plan in existence today!

401(k) Relationship Schematic

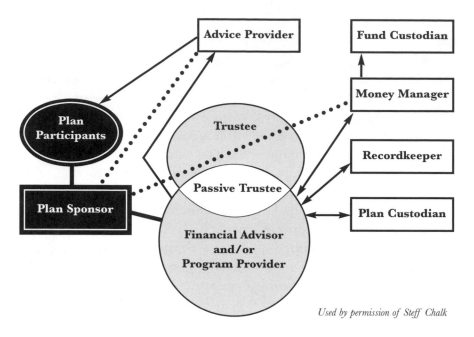

Used by permission of Steff Chalk

Relationships Between the Involved Parties

- There is a direct relationship between the plan sponsor and plan participants
- There is a direct relationship between the plan sponsor and the Financial Advisor and/or program provider
- There is usually a direct relationship between the plan participants and the advice provider
- There is usually an indirect relationship between the plan sponsor and the money managers
- There is usually an indirect relationship between the plan sponsor and the advice provider
- There is usually a direct relationship between the Financial Advisor and/or program provider and the money managers
- There is usually an indirect relationship between the Financial Advisor and/or program provider and the advice provider
- There is usually a direct relationship between the Financial Advisor and/or program provider and the recordkeeper
- There is usually a direct relationship between the Financial Advisor and/or program provider and the custodian of the plan
- There is usually a direct relationship between the money manager and the fund custodian

Explanation of Schematic

Plan Participants (benefactor) — The plan participants receive economic benefit from their employer's delivery of a strong retirement plan.

Plan Sponsor (benefactor) — The plan benefits the sponsoring company by helping the company to attract, retain, reward and motivate long-term employees.

Trustee Service Provider — There is no consistency throughout the industry regarding the duties and responsibilities of a full trustee or a directed trustee. Services of a trustee include an overlap of fiduciary responsibility. Trustees do have a fiduciary responsibility to the plan and its participants, however all involved fiduciaries are not necessarily trustees. Be aware of the term "directed trustee" or "passive trustee." These terms indicate a limited commitment to both plan sponsors and plan participants on the part of the trustee. You will note that many of the other relationships in a 401(k) program pass through the trustee realm. This includes the money manager and can include the investment advice provider. It is the plan sponsor who actually selects, hires and employs the providers. Therefore the plan sponsor is held accountable for the quality of service being delivered to plan participants. A plan sponsor with their head in the sand has his backside fully exposed.

Financial Advisor and/or Program Provider — The Financial Advisor and/or program provider is the selling firm or relationship firm. They generate economic benefit for their own firm by closing, servicing and maintaining the business relationship with the plan sponsor.

Investment Advice Provider — These relationships are not consistently structured throughout the industry. In some cases these relationships are determined by the plan sponsor and in others by the primary vendor or direct program provider. The investment advice provider can be hired by the plan sponsor, the program provider or in some cases even the plan participant. Regardless of who hires the investment advice provider, there is a relationship established between the investment advice provider and the plan participants. There is usually an indirect or direct link between the advice provider and the plan sponsor.

Money Manager — The money manager is usually positioned by or hired by the program provider.

Fund Custodian(s) — The entity responsible for holding the plan assets at the fund level.

Recordkeeper — The entity which maintains participant account balances for the benefit of the plan and plan participants.

Custodian of the Plan — The Trustee which holds plan assets.

Appendix D

— Index of Questions —

Section I – Building Your Brand

Chapter 1 – Self-Assessment

Q. 1   What did you do before becoming a Financial Advisor?

Q. 2   What experiences (both personal and professional) are "milestones" that define you?

Q. 3   What past career experiences will assist you in the role of a Financial Advisor?

Q. 4   What is your annual 401(k)/Company Retirement Plan Business revenue?

Q. 5   Prepare an inventory of your current 401(k)/Company Retirement Plans, and all other employer-sponsored retirement savings plans.

Q. 6   In what percentage of your current 401(k)/Company Retirement Plan business was there a prior relationship with the decision maker(s) and or company?

Q. 7   What are the primary reasons you were successful in winning your current plans?

Q. 8   Describe the structure of your business (solo or team or something else). If you have a team, outline/describe team member responsibilities.

Q. 9   Do you have a current Business Plan?

Q. 10   Do you feel that you fully understand all that you (or your team) have to offer and deliver to clients — all of the talents and resources that each of your team members can provide?

Q. 11   What monumental obstacles keep you from being a success in your job?

Q. 12   What are your exceptional skills?

Q. 13   What makes you or your team different than the competition?

Q. 14   What are your greatest opportunities for improvement in the 401(k)/Company Retirement Plan marketplace?

Q. 15   At what level of your organization will you brand?

Q. 16   What should you create and what should you purchase?

Q. 17   How much "psychology of selling" will your sales process incorporate?

Chapter 2 — Looking Forward

Q. 18   What is your team Vision?

Q. 19   What is your team Mission?

Q. 20   What are your team Values?

Q. 21   What is the appropriate process for establishing the Vision statement?

Q. 22   What is the best way to begin a session for developing our Vision-Mission-Values?

Q. 23   What key questions should I ask in order to develop my organizational (or team) Vision, Mission and Values?

Q. 24   Where should I focus my efforts?

Q. 25   Do you (or your team) have biases?

Q. 26   When asked by a plan sponsor to explain why you (your team) should be considered to service their company retirement savings plan, how would you respond?

Q. 27   What should I do if the response from our team is not consistent?

Chapter 3 — Your Strategic Plan

Q. 28   What is a Strategic Plan?

Q. 29   Do I need a Strategic Plan?

Q. 30   How do I begin to develop a Strategic Plan?

Q. 31   How do I make sure that my Strategic Plan is the correct one for my team?

Q. 32   How often should I revisit and revise my Strategic Plan?

Q. 33   What should my Strategic Plan include?

Q. 34   How will my Strategic Plan be developed?

Q. 35   How do I prioritize major initiatives within my Strategic Plan?

Q. 36   What do I need to accomplish and by when?

Q. 37   How do I determine the priority of tasks?

Q. 38   Is my Strategic Plan the same as my Business Plan?

Chapter 4 — Your Business Plan

Q. 64   What should I be looking for in a contact management program?

Q. 65   How do I develop my database of prospects?

Q. 66   How should I proceed if I am new to the analysis of database and contact management software?

Q. 67   What client/prospect data should be maintained within my system?

Q. 68   Who should be responsible for entering data into the database?

Q. 69   How can I measure my progress?

Q. 70   How do I utilize the information gathered through measurement?

Q. 71   Why is the Service Agreement in both major categories of Marketing and Service?

Q. 72   Can you describe a successful Service Agreement?

Q. 73   How do I determine the type of prospects and clients that I should be working with?

Q. 74   What is the definition of a target prospect?

Q. 75   What segment of the market is your "sweet spot"?

Q. 76   Why have you identified the above as your sweet spot?

Q. 77   Have you identified which type of business you are best suited to serve?

Q. 78   What methods should I utilize to deliver my message to prospects and clients?

Q. 79   How do I develop my acquisition activities?

Q. 80   How should I contact my prospects?

Q. 81   How should I reach out to prospects?

Q. 82   What do you suggest that we provide to our prospects and clients in electronic format?

Q. 83   What do you suggest that we provide to our prospects and clients in print format?

Q. 84   What do you suggest we provide to our prospects and clients in person?

Q. 105 What traits are consistently exhibited by strong competitors in your area?

Q. 106 How do I acquire high quality competitive intelligence?

Q. 107 Can I successfully differentiate myself in the area of invest-ments when so many plan sponsors view the plan investments as a commodity?

Q. 108 Does any current news or article from a national, regional or local publication impact your competitor's relationship with their plan sponsor?

Q. 109 What resources does the competition use to stay current with the 401(k) market?

Q. 110 Describe in three sentences or less how your current program differs from each of your top three competitors.

Q. 111 How does this compare to how your competition describes their service to your prospects/clients?

Section II – Product Awareness

Chapter 7 — Basic Retirement Plan Knowledge

Q. 112 What are the major components of a retirement plan business?

Q. 113 What does design include?

Q. 114 What does administration include?

Q. 115 What does recordkeeping include?

Q. 116 What does employee communications include?

Q. 117 What is the function of a trustee?

Q. 118 How much time should I spend learning design?

Q. 119 How much time should I spend learning administration?

Q. 120 How much time should I spend learning investments?

Q. 121 How much time should I spend learning recordkeeping?

Q. 122 How much time should I spend learning employee communication?

Q. 123 How much time should I spend learning the aspects of trusteeship?

Q. 124 With so many components of 401(k)/Company Retirement Plans, how do I know where to concentrate my time?

Q. 144 What are specific plan sponsor/client needs?

Q. 145 What needs to be coordinated for a successful 401(k)/Company Retirement Plan?

Q. 146 How much time should the plan sponsors spend on managing the plan?

Q. 147 How much time should I spend educating the plan sponsor?

Q. 148 What if the client or plan sponsor will not allocate the proper attention that a 401(k)/Company Retirement Plan requires?

Q. 149 What if I notice that the plan sponsor client has breached their fiduciary duty?

Q. 150 How do I convince the client to concentrate on those components that are important to the success of the plan?

Q. 151 What if the plan sponsor/client is not reviewing the correct information but they are relying on me (and are buying my product)?

Q. 152 How do I respond if my client/prospect plan sponsor has no interest in managing the plan components?

Q. 153 How do I simplify 401(k)/Company Retirement Plan management for my client?

Q. 154 Where can I find fresh ideas?

Section III – Continuous Improvement

Chapter 10 — Getting Better

Q. 155 How do I "get better"?

Q. 156 What questions should I ask myself if my goal is to get better

Q. 157 What else I can do in my efforts to get better?

Q. 158 Should I scrap my existing system and start over?

Q. 159 Where are you weak?

Q. 160 Are those areas identified as weak currently targeted for improvement within your strategic objectives?

Q. 161 Within the areas of presentation skills, setting strategy and lead generation, where are you the weakest?

Q. 162 Do you have sufficient knowledge within this industry to help plan sponsors?

Q. 180　What continuing education requirements must you satisfy based upon your current professional designations or state and national registrations?

Q. 181　What is your plan to promote your marketplace knowledge?

Q. 182　What resources do you use to stay current with the employer-sponsored savings plan?

Q. 183　What actions will you be taking for professional development, designations, conferences, etc.

Chapter 12 — Developing Strategic Partners

Q. 184　Who might be my strategic partners?

Q. 185　Should I build my business alone or seek the assistance of others, either as strategic partners or team members?

Q. 186　What industry professional classifications should I consider including in my strategic partnership network and how can we work together?

Q. 187　Besides the direct involvement of a sale to a plan prospect, what are other ways to develop my strategic partnership network?

Q. 188　How many strategic partners do you currently work with?

Q. 189　How long have you been working with your current strategic partners?

Q. 190　Where do you (your organization or you as an individual) add value to your strategic partners?

Q. 191　What if I notice that my competition appears to have strategic partnerships that I am missing and I have not developed?

Q. 192　Should I be looking at developing new strategic partners?

Q. 193　Why use a Strategic Partnership Agreement?

Q. 194　What are the components of a Strategic Partnership Agreement?

Q. 195　Should strategic partners be involved in the sales cycle?

Q. 196　Should I be evaluating my strategic partners and our partnership arrangement on an ongoing basis?

Chapter 13 — Process

Section IV - Your Responsibility

Chapter 14 — Leadership and Strategy

Section V - Maximum Efficiency

Chapter 19 — Putting it All Together

Q. 252 How will we know if our team is moving forward and "staying the course?"

Q. 253 How do I prepare the team?

Q. 254 How do I make the team part of the solution process?

Q. 255 What is the most important aspect of attempting to attain Maximum Efficiency?